Hidden in Plain Sight

YOSHIYAHU & HULDAH DAUID

The Awakening Remnant
CALIFORNIA

Disclaimer:

Hidden in Plain Sight was prepared and accomplished by Huldah Dauid in her own personal capacity. The opinions expressed in this article are the author's own and do not reflect the view of any organization, group, or the United States government. Huldah Dauid, Yoshiyahu Dauid, and/or The Awakening Remnant Koalition are in no way affiliated with any religions or movements, included but not limited to: Christianity (in any capacity or denomination), Islam (in any capacity), Judaism (in any capacity),Black Lives Matter, Nation of Islam, Black Hebrew Israelite Movement, Hebrew Roots Movement, anti-Semitic groups, or national hate groups, etc. Huldah Dauid, Yosiyahu Dauid, and/or are not attached to any of the artists or authors mentioned, and their views on the expressed topics do not reflect the views of any individual included but not limited to: Rudolph Windsor, Ms. Lauryn Hill, Aria Nasir, Brad Scott, etc

Contents

A Message to Ms. Lauryn Hill

In the Hebrew Scriptures, Judah was not only a tribe but also the name gave to Jacob and Leah's fourth son. Leah named him Judah because her sorrow had turned joy.

And she conceived again, and bare a son: and she said, now will I praise Yahuah: therefore, she called his name Yahudah; and left bearing.

Genesis 29:35

She realized that the source of her joy was in Yah.

This word Yahudah (Judah) means praise and is from the Hebrew root יהד (Yadah), which means "to throw" or "cast forth" the hands in praise and confession. It is the voice of Judah that will bring the necessary praise and confession, which will break the chains of bondage placed on the children of Yah by breaking His covenant. This tribe later turns into a nation of people with a unique purpose. The Children of Judah's praise is an essential element to Elohim's Family and their awakening. They are the voice that brings truth to future generations. It is Judah's Roar that moves his people; it's the voice of Judah's descendants that shake the faulty foundations built by their adversaries. The lion's roar breaks the chain of systemic oppression and mental bondage.

The voice of Ms. Lauryn Hill, a Lioness of Judah, has echoed forth with the same veracity of her ancestors, breaking the mental bondage off of generations of people worldwide. Her voice and boldness evoke praise and confession, which is the beginning of true freedom. Ms. Hill has the type of voice that compelled Me, a young woman, born in central California to reevaluate her whole outlook on life and truth. She challenged me to *Rebel, rock with the 144, forgive them father*, and to *keep my eye on the final hour*. It was her voice that became my companion as *I searched the chapters and checked verses*. As I became frustrated, it was her lyrics that led me to the *73rd Psalm* which assured me that the foundations of the wicked are a slippery slope and that in the end, *it all falls down*. It was her bold, fearless stance on emancipation through the proclamation of truth that has me writing my second book with the hope of leaving a legacy of liberation to the next generation.

Many artists take for granted or abuse the influence they have on the youth. Their lyrics, whether they are conscious of it or not, shape the future. The Creator has entrusted them with a gift and influence to be used to His Glory, yet many fail to call the wayward home and shed liberating light. They do not know that the thoughts and expressions of the artist become the motive and conviction of the young impressionable minds that trust them.

While I dare not speak for everyone, I can honestly say that Ms. Lauryn Hill has done her due diligence as an artist, and has awakened a roaring lioness in me. Her level of conviction and strength through adversity has given me a double portion of boldness. She has taught me that freedom beings within, and that a voice is more powerful than a million weapons. Whether she knows it or not, she is a Prophetess. Her words and lyrics have assisted in awakening a generation who see the importance of emitting truth into the universe to combat the lies of the powers- that-be, and the systems that they have set in place. It is the root from the SEED of Jesse and the spirit of the Everlasting and Eternal that resonates through her. A wise person once told me that you cannot un-ring a bell, and what Ms. Hill has done through her music has vibrated into my soul. I am humbled and blessed that the Father allowed me to catch the frequency of His truth in her lyrics. While I do not know her or where her life has taken her, if I ever got the opportunity to say something to her it would be thank you. Thank you for your obedience, and rest assured that your work was/is not done in vain.

Respectfully,

Huldah Dauid

Dedication

This book is dedicated to the scattered and dispersed and their companions. Because of the nature of the book and the perspective of the authors, which is based in a Western Hemispheric setting we want to assure the readers, that the other tribes around the world have not been overlooked. Thus we want to recognize the Bantu people, the Maasai, the Tutsi, Lemba and other African Tribes who are a part of the scatter and dispersed of Israel and Judah due to the Diaspora. We also want to recognize other unacknowledged/or unknown tribes and groups worldwide and their companions who are also awaiting their revelation, and redemption. May we solicit the prayers of all Yah's children in every country, who are awaiting the awakening of Judah and Israel to their covenant obligation of obedience, to mobilize back home.

To the Remnant, you have not been forgotten, and your faithfulness is how we were able to find our markers in this strange land which helped us to reclaim our culture. Until we are gathered into our land may Yah keep you. And NEVER forget YAH is on OUR side!

Psalm 124

If it had not been Yahuah who was on our side, now may Israel say;

> *If it had not been Yahuah who was on our side, when men rose up against us:*
>
> *Then they had swallowed us up quick, when their wrath was kindled against us:*
>
> *Then the waters had overwhelmed us, the stream had gone over our soul:*
>
> *Then the proud waters had gone over our soul.*
>
> *Blessed be Yahuah, who hath not given us as a prey to their teeth.*
>
> *Our soul is escaped as a bird out of the snare of the fowlers: the snare is broken, and we are escaped.*
>
> *Our help is in the name of Yahuah, who made heaven and earth.*

By what authority do we do the majority hasn't a clue
We majored in curses search the chapters check the verses
Recapture the land and remove the mark from off our hand
So we can stand in agreement with HIS command
Everything else is damned let them with ears understand!

—Ms. Lauryn Hill *(War in the Mind)*

Introduction

Throughout history, there has been a mission of the powers-that-be to cover and suppress the true identity of the "African-American" people. The reason for this is the undeniably strong historical connection between the identity of the Hebrew Israelites of the Southern Kingdom and the people who live in the Americas and other regions around the world. The identity of the original Israelite people is becoming a heavily debated issue amongst ecclesiastical bodies and conscious communities because of a mass awakening of individuals who have begun studying ancient texts and parallels found in Scriptures between themselves and the Hebrew Israelite people of antiquity.

In academia and circles of scholarship, there is the apparent effort to tip-toe around the facts to cause people to walk away with an attitude of ambiguity to one of the most important matters that has presented itself to humanity in recent centuries.

1

The question implored is rather straight forward and attainable, and that is, who are the real Chosen People that the Bible speaks of and are they still relevant today? By denying the world this answer in veritable scholarship, a huge problem is brewing that is spinning society out of control. This denial of truth is destroying the very fabric of our universe and blocking the Light that can tear down racial and other divisive ideologies. Because of this suppression the issue of "why?" cannot be shaken from the minds of those who have searched out the topic of the identity of the African Americans and their connection to the Biblical characters and ancestors. Has the whole world been deceived? Can it be possible, or even true, that the whole world has fallen victim to the theft of a nation's identity, thus confirming an ersatz culture and people, and in turn disinheriting the incontrovertible Chosen People?

While many will choose to view this argument as an anti-Semitic effort to propagate another conspiracy theory against "the Chosen People of G-d," that would be furthest from truth. There is an obvious pattern through a Biblical and historical survey, from the time of the Kings to the Book of the Revelation, that reveals the replacement of Yah's people. Due to this conspiracy, the Creator has constantly had to preserve a remnant of His people to keep other nations from living as if He has abandoned His promise to redeem and draw His chosen from the four corners of the Earth.

Many nations have bought the lie that all of the prophecies and truth regarding the identity and the promises of the Hebrew people are fulfilled, yet negate to provide substantial evidence through Biblical and historical congruity which can validate the claim. With this being so, it is important to shed light on how Yahuah's covenant (with a literal people group) is still in effect and how this particular people group (or seed) has begun to show evidence through their fruit all over the world, especially in the United States of America. These same people, due to their disobedience, are currently disinherited; yet still, exist and are coming together in these modern times as dry bones to call the rest of His family, both blood-borne and grafted, to the true identity of His people and the original intent of His Word.

The present concern of denial and continued covering of His people is a familiar spirit, and the attitude of the nations is consistent with Scripture. The Bible and its prophecies fit those to whom it was entrusted to and written about. With close consideration, it will become overwhelmingly evident that the things which Scripture speaks of will continue to manifest themselves in revealing the true sons and daughters of the Highest. In discussing who the Children of Israel are, it is imperative to consider the conspiracy, the prophecy, and the importance of their revelation today. While this discussion can seem contentious, rest assured that this topic is handled with much care and consideration.

Part I

The Problem

[א]

Benefactors of Racism

"Is Israel a slave, or was he born a servant? Why then has he become plunder?" ~Jeremiah 2:14

Before tackling the topic of revealing the chosen of Yah in America, one paramount question must be answered, and that is; what difference does it make? Aren't we all one in Messiah? Over the years this has been the first question asked by individuals who are either choosing to identify with another people group as Israel or see the argument of revealing who the Chosen[1] People are as a topic rooted in divisive arrogance. Therefore, it is important to answer this question and also be

---

[1] Using historical and Scriptural evidences. Not simply believing the status quo.

sensitive to those who are seeking the Father's face on this matter. In being aware of the disputation which may arise, this cannot cause omission of veracities that ought to be presented to refine the commonly accepted interpretation of the roots racism and the material that aids its subsistence.

To answer the question in regards to the advantage of exploring information on the Chosen People, it is very simple; it did not make a difference until someone covered up the truth. Nothing becomes an issue until someone decides to beguile a whole generation with the purpose of exchanging the truth for a lie. Many people, no matter how they genealogically identify, have a negative view of Blacks, even Blacks themselves. Blacks have experienced so much racial inferiority that the result is often a disdain toward their skin color and a denial of their contributions to humanity before slavery. Furthermore, other nations, and especially those who identify as White, have been generationally taught to abhor the Negro for the same reason. While many would believe that this is merely the way that Yah ordained things (and even seek to back it up with

Scriptural or scientific evidence), it is not true. The system that was created to oppress, erase, and replace a particular people was profoundly rooted in fraudulent artifice and subordination as foretold in Scripture.

… *"Let us destroy the tree with its fruit, and let us cut him off from the land of the living, that his name be remembered no more."*

Jeremiah 19:11

These types of conversations are stifled and shut down because they pick at the wounds of a very sore history. It is the nature of humanity to hide from its indiscretions, and when humanity cannot hide, the next move is to downplay the extent to which other people are affected by their indiscretions. To see understand the difference racism makes one must deal with the elephant in the room. Did the world actively participate in the mass extermination of Yah's Chosen People? Once this issue is brought to the table, we can learn why this happened in the first place, and then were able to understand a systematic conspiracy of satanically-influenced racism. Pondering the source will aid many, both Black and White, in considering this controversial dispute, as well as the role each person plays in remedying the effects of its suppression.

The reason why people cannot believe that African-Americans are connected to the Biblical Hebrew Israelites is due to racism. The idea that African-Americans cannot be the chosen people of scripture is sustained on two commonly-believed myths, the perception that Blacks are the descendants of Ham (as a result of the curse of Canaan) and the idea that the curse placed on Cain was black (or dark) skin. Both the Talmud and the Midrash supports said myths. Below are two legends that speak to the origin of the curse of dark skin:

Three copulated in the ark, and they were all punished — the dog, the raven, and Ham. The dog was doomed to be tied, the raven expectorates [his seed into his mate's mouth], and Ham was smitten in his skin. [34] - Babylonian Talmud, Sanhedrin 108a

"Because you have abused me (sodomized/buggered me) in the darkness of the night, your children shall be born black and ugly... because you have twisted your head to cause me embarrassment, they shall have kinky hair and red eyes...because your lips jested at my exposure, theirs shall swell...and because you neglected my nakedness, they shall go naked with their shamefully elongated male members exposed to all to see... " (Noah, section 13)

Because of these myths, when someone mentions the visage of Messiah or the Chosen People, it is immediately met with an automatic rejection, because there is no way that Yah's Chosen People can be a cursed people. The only option then is for the chosen to be the opposite of black, which is white. This deceptive agenda bestows upon White Supremacy the un-contended right to have the chosen of Yah genetically assigned to its racial classes. While many are aware that the Holocaust was built on so-called White supremacy, the reality is that it had very little to do with "race" and very much to do with the practices and political reversal of historical evidence. What is commonly known among historians is the copious amounts of artifacts and books which were stolen during the time of WWII by the Nazis for some unknown reason. Why? Because if Elohim's chosen, through a historical survey, resembles the rest of the world, which is colored, then it fervidly thwarts the plan to divest the ancient Hebrews of their cultural identity, causing a shift in Yah's ordained leadership in the known world.

While it is evident that the Jewish people were hated, even the world's hatred toward this group is reconciled when it chose them instead of the more historically authentic Jews, who are hated even more. What many in Anglo groups have done by accepting a European looking group as the representation for the ancient Hebrew was deduce that it is better to be linked in some way to those who may be unfavorable historically than for the whole world to have a cursed group claiming to be chosen and favored of Elohim. The truth of the matter, then, is that the same people who everyone upholds as the Chosen People are the same individuals who created these lies along with their "enemy" the European extremist.

It was this fear that created a greater enemy and allegiance amongst the nations. In order to perpetuate these lies which teach that the Negro represents every negative character in Scripture and history, Satan is likened to the Black man, Cain is a Black in Biblical literature, and Ham's descendants are Black; meanwhile every other Biblical figure is portrayed as White, though the dispersion of color throughout the world proves differently.

The myth of black skin as a curse is heavily rooted in the deepest kind of racism. So deep, that people teach and repeat these myths to people of color, as though it is not extremely offensive, and as though it is true. Has anyone who holds this belief looked at its origin? This rejection of Blacks due to their skin and its rationale are not supported in Scripture. If you are doubtful or hesitant, please take a break and search for yourself.

These myths have not only caused a deep seeded "racial" divide but have also set a ripple effect throughout time that had produced strange fruit. The poisonous fruit has poisonous roots. And if they are not uprooted, it will further corrupt the moral fabric of society by allowing them to believe that this is being done with the authority of the Creator of the Universe. Would it be conscionable to believe that in some way Yah Himself is against a particular people group for no reason outside of their skin color? What is striking is how a false sign or wonder was placed on a certain group of colored people, while the truth of their identity remains covered. It is also telling that the false sign was given by the people who the world trusts to correctly interpret Scripture, because of their claimed close relationship with "G-d." In asking what difference does it make, the inquisitive mind must be open to understanding the tangled web that has been woven by religious and scientific racism throughout history.

Societal & Religious Racism

During a conference on Race, Research, and Education, African Scholar Asa G. Hilliard III alluded to the fact that the contemporary concept of "race" is grounded in Nazi[2] Germany (1999). He tells about the political link between race and how outside of personal agenda Hitler is quoted saying that "in the scientific sense there is no such thing as race." Interestingly, the main reason that the current Jewish[3] people are in the land of Israel today is because they are said to have been discriminated against and almost exterminated

---

[2] Nazi Germany is used in reference to the time preceding the holocaust and the ideology attached thereto.

[3] The ancient Israelites were not referred to as Jewish and did not follow Judaism. They were referred to as Hebrew or Israelites (or some variation). A Jew was from the tribe of Judah, living in the Kingdom of Judah, or Jerusalem.

due to their racial affiliation. Hitler continues with "...which enables the order which has hitherto existed and a historical basis to be abolished and an entirely new and anti-historical order enforced and given such an intellectual basis...With the conception of race, national socialism will carry its revolution abroad and recast the world." In this statement, three keywords stand out: abolish, anti-historical, and recast. Abolishing a historical basis erased the notion that people have an ancient and central origin. This adaptation gave way to duel creations and other discriminatory rhetoric that negated a common ancestor for humanity.

Next, in creating an anti-historical order on an intellectual basis, it allowed those who were in power the liberty to rewrite history without considering any historical basis, thus creating the attitude of "If I say so, it is what it is, because I make the rules." Ambiguity takes away truth and allows a description based on personally defined variables. Finally, the coup de grace was to recast the world. As Shakespeare once said, "the world is a stage and men and women merely players." In a stage play the best person for the role is cast, in biased History, this is not true. In biased history the roles are cast to perpetuate agenda. If the "cast" does not fit what society wants, there can be understudies and replacements. The error in this way of thinking is that it Implies the roles set out in the universe can be changed depending on time or as theologically stated "dispensations." Through this scheme the plan was to abolish historical truth which would link people to land and ancestors, replace these people based upon what a person says, and not what they can prove genetically or historically; which in the end places new people in the starring role of humanity for power and control of the world.

While racism cannot be entirely attributed to Hitler in its modern construct, what can be seen are the parallels of its usage. The model he used against Jews, was based on the finished prototype that was first used against the so-called Negroes. The system that removed the identity of one people through slavery and scientific racism, also was used to create a perfect environment which afforded another people to use Hitler's discrimination to grab hold of an identity that was stolen by the folklore of the Jewish commentaries.

Religious Racism

Before the claims of the curse of Cain and Ham, most people were slaves or socially out-casted based upon societal issues and not a direct correlation to black skin. It was a very common to identify the physical features of other nations, yet these differences were not used as a tool to classify a person into categories of inferiority. Also, it was common knowledge that the vast majority of the planet shared physical similarities.

Racism is a learned behavior. No one is born racist, but instead, are nurtured with certain ideologies that disseminate through young impressionable minds. The idea of superiority is passed down from generation-to-generation as a part of a strategic plan against the Negro. Of course, many will disagree and claim that other groups are discriminated against, or that other people have been mistreated for not fitting into the Western societal norms too. While these claims are indisputable, the system in place both then and now was specifically targeted against the so-called Negro. It is evident that racism exists in different forms. However, significant attention should be paid to the fact that although racism is real, even those who are oppressed find it necessary to oppress the Blacks around them. This global disdain is not only in society but has also reached the parish and the pulpit, where those who are supposed to see with the eyes of "Yahuah" are equally oppressive and supportive of this universal position of a cursed group of people.

The idea of racism as it has been experienced, as an accessory to the justification of stealing and enslaving unwilling individuals, is foreign not only to Scripture but also to history. In ancient times the enslavement of people was drastically different from today and was not motivated by scientific stigma or fabricated folklore created by religious dogma. Race and its ideology about human differences arose out of the context folklore and was advanced in the preaching of Judeo-Christian theologians who used passed-down myths from the Jewish and other Europeans to justify the enslavement of who they were led to believe were cursed individuals who "Elohim" had placed on the planet to be servants to the "chosen" race.

Carroll, Charles. Adam and Eve. 1900. The Negro a Beast. St. Louis, Missouri, 1900. 2, 21, & 62. Print

(Davis, 2008, p. 32)

One might argue that racism was in the Bible, but would be hard-pressed to substantiate the claim. Torah never speaks of discriminating against a person for any physical (non-medically harmful) reason. All of Scripture is based on an allegiance to Yah. While this is the true interpretation of the Torah, it has been grossly used as a discriminatory act against Yah's people. The Jewish people who claim to be the chosen of Yah have used Torah, and their interpretation of it, as a vehicle to exclude people from the covenant of Yah. This discrimination has been passed down and evolved into an accessory to slavery and modern-day racism.

The system of separation justified by scientific and religious authorities created a perfect storm for a permanent caste system for blacks. The ramifications of their system made it impossible, even after slavery, for blacks to assimilate into society even through the benevolence of Elohim. A group of social untouchables whom even the chosen of the Highest enslaved and hated. One very disturbing quote comes at the hand of a Rabbi during slavery who speaks of the "African" as servants by divine ordination which gives justification to Christians who needed confirmation for their obscure viewpoints on slavery. By dehumanizing the negro, oppression, enslavement, and mistreatment is justified. Sadly, this same view has roots in lots of today's Messianic or Hebrew Roots groups. These subconscious ideologies are a driving force of biased actions and the aversion to the negro as anything higher than a servant. While many don't know where these passed down heresies came from, they can be found all throughout history in the writings of slave owners, theologians, and even rabbis. One particular rabbi is quoted in the Jewish Record of January 23, 1863 speaking on the comparison between the Negro and the Israelite:

"We know not how to speak in the same breath of the Negro and the Israelite. The very names have startlingly opposite sounds — one representing all that is debased and inferior in the hopeless barbarity and heathenism of six thousand years; the other, the days when Jehovah conferred on our fathers the

glorious equality which led the Eternal to converse with them and allow them to enjoy the communion of angels. Thus the abandoned fanatics insult the choice of Elohim himself, in endeavoring to reverse the inferiority which he stamped on the African, to make him the compeer, even in bondage, of His Chosen People. There is no parallel between such races. Humanity from pole to pole would scout such a comparison. The Hebrew was originally free, and the charter of his liberty was inspired by his Creator. The Negro was never free, and his bondage in Africa was simply duplicated in a milder form when he was imported here.... The judicious in all the earth agree that to proclaim the African equal to the surrounding races, would be a farce which would lead the civilized conservatism of the world to denounce the outrage. "(Sicher, 2013)

This view is not isolated, but is echoed by Jew and Christian alike throughout the Western world about the "African" or the "Negro" in its midst. The mark of servitude was said to be so grievous that even upon conversion to Christianity the Negro would still not have his status as a slave or as a beast (2/3 a human) changed. The Negro, no matter how "repentant," would keep the "curse" of black skin upon him. The endorsed process of changing the visage of a whole continent of people to a tag for bondage and mistreatment went from being folklore or legend to a doctrine that would follow a people to modern time. The issue of history and racial origin is changed to justify racism blatantly.

Reverse Racism

Most people who are willing to call out the Jewish as well as other Europeans on both their deceptive and racist past, are confronted and attacked with reverse-racism. The idea of reverse-racism is a ridiculous claim made by racists or descendants of slave owners and benefactors of the subservient position placed on Negros, who feel as though by being pro-black, somehow the so-called Negro is anti-White. For the record, it is impossible to be a reverse racist when the underlying factors are not present.

It would take a proper amount of influence and leverage to significantly change the position of White Supremacy to stake that claim; and it is overwhelmingly evident that the Black community, due to systemic repression and oppression, lacks the influence to reduce or eliminate White privilege and its benefactors. When any Negro, regardless of capacity, expresses disdain for his/her treatment in this country, it occurs from the weariness of always climbing uphill to create a place in a system hell-bent against them and their ethnic identity. Blacks do not view White people and innately gain displeasure. Rather, the displeasure that Blacks do hold is merely due to the actions of the whole group, and not the white skin on its own.

The main reason Blacks are frustrated with Whites is because of the negligent behavior that facilitates and promulgates repetitive behaviors of exploitation that have damaged their community. Unfortunately, this is not a small sample of actions, but the overall attitude and rhetoric of the Western nations as a whole. It can be overtly seen in their confederate flags and reverence of a nation built on the backs of involuntary slaves. Also, it can be more covert in the form of silence when their counterparts carry out the deep-seeded hatred that is intricately woven into the Western, American capitalist society.

Race and its ideology about human differences arose out of the context of the justification of "African" enslavement. But many people throughout history have been enslaved without the imposition of racial ideology. Interestingly the foundation for racism had already been proven to be tried and true in demeaning and degrading one group of people. Through the catalyst of Nazi Germany, racism by nationality would contribute to the birth (or as some believe the rebirth) of a nation who are no longer historically linked, but rather intellectual linked to the Israelites. The same racism that was used to disinherit one group is used to hand over the identity and authority to another group.

By believing these racist indoctrinations, whether Black, Jewish, White, etc. a person is becoming an active participant in a lie that is the root of all racial divide. Telling the truth about these issues is not what is dividing us. Returning the inheritance of a people from which it was stolen is not contentious, but rather maintaining the status quo although it has had large holes placed in its logic is the real issue. Instead of reversing injustices, many have chosen to hold on to biased thought and divisive ideologies that continue to broaden the gulf of racial division. The remedy cannot be more of the same. Has the whole world become insane? Society is repeating the cycles of old in order to create new hope. Insanity! What humanity must seek to do is eradicate the mental chains which have been placed on it due to ignorance and naivety created by skin color bias and deep seeded hatred and racism. Mankind often trusts those in authority to its detriment. The whole world has allowed the sins of divisive powers and wicked forefathers to disinherit them of their blessings. This is both foolish and sad. Any biased thoughts that support the removal of markers, history, and suppresses truth are not of the Father, but of the adversary.

If the foundation of a house is not built on truth, then the whole house will fall. America and

Western civilization is built on a sandy foundation and as the rain begins to pour because of lies and myths the damage will be evident of such. Western Civilization will not be saved, like Egypt, Babylon, and Rome it will see a similar fate. The world system that is known spiritually as Babylon and Sodom has sealed her fate and those who call themselves believers must come out of it both physically and mentally. The doctrines of Babylon are what cause our divide. The truth of the Scriptures, no matter how opposed to one's central way of thinking, is what will unify. Humanity must seek to have its mind renewed and cleansed of the weeds of the adversary which so easily beset and divide us. To continue to allow these lies to shape how one thinks and reacts to blacks without truly searching out the Father's heart in this matter could potentially be the greatest mistake humanity will ever make. While the house cannot be saved the souls inside are being given the opportunity to be redeemed from the sins of their forefathers.

Part II

The Cause

[ג]

The Seed [4]

One might argue that racism was in the Bible, but would be hard-pressed to substantiate the claim. Torah never speaks of discriminating against those who are willing to identify with the SEED, and it also doesn't allow the negation of the physical SEED by those who find refuge in the "grace" of the camp. The Bible clearly explains, confirms, and in no uncertain terms shows through all of its pages the importance of the Hebrew people; not only to the Creator but the whole world because of their purpose of unify and lighting the way to Yahuah. To understand the function of the

---

[4] Genealogy charts are on page 233. These charts prove that the So-Called Negro is not a Gentile. Anglo- Religion teaches that the Negros are Gentiles, but they are by curses, and historical evidence Shemites and more specifically a portion of the Israelites mentioned in Scripture.

Chosen People as whole, and Judah (as the leader of the Tribes) who this book claim is heavily represented by so called Negros in the Americas and abroad, there must first be a foundation laid for how and why prophecy is used throughout the pages of Scripture. In order to substantiate these claims defining what prophecy is and why it is important to understanding Scripture is a major key. This Key will open the vaults of knowledge and unlock the suppressed minds to reveal who Judah is. The identification of Judah will shed light on identifying Israel, and finally will help those who are grafted in as family and companions understand their rights and inheritance within the family.

The Hebrew word for prophecy is נבא (neb-oo-aw). The meaning of this word in the original language gives us the heart of Yah for His people and the original intent for prophecy. The word is composed of a 2-letter root נב. The *nun* is a picture of a seed, and the *bet* is a picture of a tent, house, or that which is inside. When these meanings are combined, we see the pictographical definition of "seed inside." This is a very beautiful definition of prophecy and the nation of Israel; within the house is the seed. The house is representative of the set-apart place for the family. While the house may host a stranger or a sojourner, the house still only produces the seed that is similar to the original intent of the fruit. Prophecy is a picture of fruit that is produced from inside. The seed is the Word, and when that Word is planted by the Father, it produces a tree that bears fruit. The tree spoken of in Scripture is Israel, and the knowledge (fruit) of that tree should bear witness of the Father, and likewise the Father uses the tree to bring and nourish others by the seed of truth. Thus the function of prophecy is for the nation of Israel to reveal the seed inside which is the Word.

Throughout the history of Torah and the Tanakh, there are prophets called to bring forth the inner seed. In this book, the same pattern is followed in uncovering the truth and function of the House of Judah and their companions. The pattern is to show the seed inside so that the fruit can be judged. According to the laws of observational evidence in Torah, a seed has to bear fruit after its kind; first physically, and then spiritually.

The Children of Israel were first a physical seed through Abraham. Next, they became a spiritual seed by their deeds and commitment to following Yahuah; but what never changes are their original purpose. No other nation or religious denomination can claim to be from this tree, yet not exemplify the fruit after the original kind.

And Elohim said, Let the earth bring forth grass, the herb yielding seed, and the fruit-tree yielding fruit after his kind, whose seed is in itself, upon the earth: and it was so.

Genesis 1:11

Likewise, every functional tree bears functional fruit, but a dysfunctional tree bears dysfunctional fruit.

Matthew 7:18

Through prophecy in the Word and close examination of the fruit which comes forth from that seed, one can determine who the Hebrews were to Yah and how important the House of Judah is in tandem with the restoration of Israel and their companions today.

As previously stated, there has been a conspiracy; and even Scripture speaks of it as such. In Psalm 83:4 the writer declares that the nations have come together to *kahad*, or hide the Children of Israel so that their names and the remembrance of them will be no more. If ever a person has wondered why it is so difficult to explain who the

Children of Israel are, this is why. The information has constantly been hidden and blurred by those who have joined in the effort to cut these particular people off from being a nation. With that little nugget, we will explore just how these types of prophecies have never happened to anyone else. There are only one people on the planet who have a concealed identity marred by the united forces of various nations through a curse that would be given thousands of years in advanced, but it is also the divine providential care of the Creator to keep a remnant who will manifest and fulfill these words in the last days. Let's look at the truth behind who identifies as the true chosen of Yah.

One issue that has made it hard to identify the Hebrew people throughout history is the inconsistency of Western scholars when handling the Bible in connection with historical evidence. It has been the practice of these so-called theologians or historians to isolate the Biblical characters from the historical world. Through research Biblically and extra-Biblically, there is a close-knit correlation between the characters of the Bible and every major leader and nation in history. One of the reasons why the correlation between historical and Biblical cultures and figures are not easily seen is because of the language of the ruling power and the patriarchs and the people being nomads or sojourners in that land. Consider this thought: If people 2,000 years from now researched America they would never know that tribes of the Hebrew people were enslaved here because they would be looking for Hebrews, whereas here they are referred to as either Black or African-American. Someone would have to open their eyes to the connection, and even then for many that would be a hard bridge to cross. Because this is true in searching for the original people and their journey to their current situation, it is imperative to begin before Israel existed as a nation.

[ד]

The Connection

The Hebrew people have origins in the first civilization. Due to a misunderstanding of the Biblical and secular historical connection many people place the Hebrew people in Egypt and forget that the very first Hebrews had their roots in Sumer. Sumer, Biblically referred to as Shinar, a place called Ur, is where everything bottle-necks. While there were several civilizations in this period, Sumer is where the post-diluvian (flood) world begins to flourish again as a whole. This place is home to the first major tribal confederation after the flood under the leadership of a Hamite by the name of Nimrod. Nimrod descends from Noah's son, Ham, who was one of the three sons who disembarked the ark after the Great Flood.

(The other two sons were named Shem and Japheth). It is through these three sons that we have the first three tribal divisions that will later account for the rest of the world as written in Genesis 10. We will focus on Nimrod to make a historical and cultural connection that has also been hidden to invalidate the historical accuracy of the Bible. One of the arguments about Biblical accuracy is that it does not mention world leaders that would have been present during the time Scripture claims Hebrews were in various cities. One of the greatest leaders of history, who is given the title of the first major lawgiver is Hammurabi. It is believed that Hammurabi lived in a similar period as Abram, yet Scripture does not mention the existence of this character, thus negating his role in Sumer where Abram lives. The reason for this oversight has to do with something as "simple" as a name. Hammurabi is not the original name of this punitive lawgiver. Scripture calls him by the name of Amraphel or Ammuraphi, king of Shinar. In the book of Jasher (Jasher 11:16) we find out that the king Amraphel is none other than Nimrod who experienced a name change after the fall of the

Tower of Babel. Just like Nimrod's name change hid the connection between Hammurabi, Shinar, and the patriarch Abraham, leaving room for speculation and dialogue about the inaccuracy of Scripture, the same applies to the Hebrew people.

This same formula has been used to conceal the original Hebrews of the Bible. Not only is their existence essential to humanity now, but it was then also. This issue is the name of the people. The name Hebrew (Ivri) as an identifying marker on a people goes back before Abraham to a descendent by the name of Eber (Ever), who descends from the line of Shem. In Shem's lineage, the patriarch Abraham is born and he is the first person in Scripture who is called a Hebrew by name. His tribal name is ascribed, and all of his descendants are called by this name as well. Hebrews or Bnei Eber break into several tribes that make up the Hebrew people. Because of several tribes and their divisions, there are various names for the Hebrew family early in history. They are called Haburu, habbat (bandit, robber, or raider) Hapiri (soldiers from the West), Apiru, Habiru (nomadic invaders), and Shashu. It is not until the Sons of Jacob that the world is introduced to a chosen family group that will later enter a nation of bondage in order to come out a great multitude through the providential care of the Highest. It will later be through the promise to Abraham and through the faithfulness of this particular family group that the blessing of the whole world will come.

It is also evident that the 12 tribes of Israel do not represent all the Hebrews, but rather the avenue of choice for salvation to the world. At this point, many may want to know what is so important about this one family in comparison to all the other Hebrews that Yah had to choose from between Eber and Abraham. The Covenant stand on the obedience and the response these two patriarchs made to the character call of a Hebrew, which means "to cross over." Many Hebrews are unwilling to take the steps required to cross over, and this is why the Highest chooses to make His covenant with a remnant who carry the seed of the house and not with those who manipulate the seed and bear strange fruit. In history, when Israel bore fruit contrary to what was laid out in their Covenant, they were cut off. The same applies to any tree claiming to be of the Father, yet bearing a fruit that does not fit the Covenant established with the seed of Abraham and specifically the 12 tribes of Israel.

Because Elohim chooses a people and this theme continues throughout the Biblical narrative, many believe it is unfair. Some also think that this somehow taints the ability of Elohim to love anyone else. The truth of the matter is that it is in the Highest's love that He does all things; including His choice of a people above all other people to carry out a plan that would in turn benefit all those who were willing to accept and follow His people as they followed Him. This choice was not an afterthought, although all nations had the chance to receive His law through the testimony of His servants. This plan was laid out at Creation. By the very creative act of shaping the worlds, Elohim had the authority to choose (from that creation) a people who would be a light to others; because He knows better than us and we have no right to question His authority. Scripture tells us that the Highest did not choose Israel because of them, but rather because of the Promise and Covenant with the seed which is housed within Israel.

> *"Yahuah loved you and chose you not because of your great number exceeding all other peoples, for you are fewer than all of the peoples, but because of the love of Yahuah for you and because of his keeping of the sworn oath that he swore to your ancestors, Yahuah brought you out with a strong hand and redeemed you from the house of slavery, from the hand of Pharaoh, the king of Egypt.*

Deuteronomy 7:7-8

Yah's Connection to the Physical SEED?

The relationship between Israel and their Elohim is unique when compared to other belief systems. Most religions choose their gods, but this is not so with Israel, as previously stated in Deut 7:7-8; He chose them. The Highest Elohim did not want to just be a "god" to Israel like other nations; He chose to be their Father. Father in Hebrew is

אב. The *Aleph* is the strong leader, the ox, and the source; while the *bet* is the house. The relationship between Israel and Yah is that He is the Source and Leader of the house. There is a second picture in this combination that is revealed in its numerical value of three (adding the *aleph* and *bet* together) which symbolizes fresh fruit and is representative of the next generation of trees currently housed in the fruit bore from the original tree. This imagery teaches how those who are a part of the original tree are supposed to be related to the Source. The physical is established to show evidence of that which is spiritual. Thus, the physical Chosen People are proof of a spiritual people. If the physical is removed or disregarded, then there is no hope for those who want to join the family spiritually. If Yah has not kept His promise to the physical seed and preserved their existence, as He has promised, then there is also no sure hope for those who claim to be grafted in or from the spiritual seed. The marker of the original tree is necessary for all those who want to claim a position in the family through the process of being grafted. Rabbi Shaul spoke about the importance of the evidence of the things unseen:

> *Now faith is the substance of things hoped for, the evidence of things not seen.*
>
> Hebrews 11:1

The things that are seen have its source in the strong leader who gave of His seed continue or secure the life of the family. To understand who the Chosen People are, one must trace the seed back to two places; the physical father and the spiritual father. Contrary to popular belief, both fathers matter; and it is often Yah, the spiritual Father who chooses the physical one. Most people decide to ignore the fact that Yah houses His spiritual seed in physical vessels. The tendency is to separate the two, while a person can become the spiritual seed and not be of the physical seed; a family member of the physical seed cannot represent the family of faith without the spiritual seed. Another interesting concept in Torah is that the bloodline of the adopted is not differentiated from that of the blood-born. One would not be able to tell any difference between the biological and the adopted through a proper grafting process. Both are called by the Father, and this is an important picture because Yah not only chooses a natural seed, but also the place in which He plants the seed.

It is the faith of the patriarchs from this physical family and their descendants who bring salvation and redemption to the whole house. This is not a single effort, but a combination of the Father's SEED and the chosen physical seed. The physical tree is the faith or the observable witness to the spiritual seed. It is the same seed from the beginning. The Highest speaks of this seed as an ancient people, and as a people who are near to His heart and He will not forget the physical seed from their ancestors.

Can a woman forget her sucking child, that she should not have compassion on the son of her womb? Yea, they may forget, yet will I not forget thee. 16Behold, I have graven thee upon the palms of my hands; thy walls are continually before me. Thy children shall make haste; thy destroyers and they that made thee waste shall go forth of thee.

Isaiah 49:15-17

The Highest has a critical line in this passage, found at the end of Verse 15. He states that "Yea, they may forget, yet will I not forget thee." Other nations have forgotten the elect of the Highest because of the crafty counsel of those aforementioned in Psalm 83, but the Highest goes to great lengths to ensure that His people are not forgotten, to the point that He anthropomorphically speaks of engraving them on His palms.

Remember these, O Jacob and Israel; for thou art my servant: I have formed thee; thou art my servant: O

*Israel, thou shalt not be forgotten of me. I have
blotted out, as a thick cloud, thy transgressions, and,
as a cloud, thy sins: return unto me; for I have
redeemed thee.*

Isaiah 44:21-22

In these verses and several others throughout
Scripture, the Father uses the names Jacob and
Israel. At first glance, this seems to be rather
redundant, but under careful examination, this can
be understood as a distinction between his physical
and the spiritual. Jacob's name means supplanter,
and it deals with his physical nature, but when his
named was changed to Israel, it was because of a
spiritual nature that he exhibited when he "strove
with Yah" (Gen. 35:10). The character of both seeds
is still seen in one man and one family. If that is not
enough to see that the spiritual and the physical
must be one, then look at the verses where Yah
speaks of Jacob's seed and how they will be
preserved forever.

*"And their seed shall be known among the Gentiles,
and their offspring among the people: all that see*

them shall acknowledge them, that they are the seed which Yahuah hath blessed."

Isaiah 61:9

O Lord, why hast thou made us to err from thy ways, and hardened our heart from thy fear? Return for thy servants' sake, the tribes of thine inheritance.

Isaiah 63:17

And I will bring forth a seed out of Jacob, and out of Judah an inheritor of my mountains: and mine elect shall inherit it, and my servants shall dwell there.

Isaiah 65:9

For as the new heavens and the new earth, which I will make, shall remain before me, saith Yahuah, so shall your seed and your name remain.

Isaiah 66:22

I will cause thee to ride upon the high places of the earth, and feed thee with the heritage of Jacob thy father: for the mouth of Yahuah hath spoken it."

Isaiah 58:12-14

In a lot of theological circles these verses are explained to mean that the blessings of Israel are through the seed of Abraham (spiritually), and that man's seed (physical) is insignificant to Yah; yet in the verses above, not only does Yah have a spiritual seed, but He also will bless the children who call Jacob their father. The 12 physical tribes of Israel are still precious in the sight of Yah, so much so that He compares His covenant with the earth after the flood, the fixed positions of the mountains and the hills to His covenant with His ancient people.

For the mountains shall depart, and the hills be removed; but my kindness shall not depart from thee, neither shall the covenant of my peace be removed, saith the Lord that hath mercy on thee

Isaiah 54:10

For I will pour water upon him that is thirsty, and floods upon the dry ground: I will pour my spirit upon thy seed, and my blessing upon thine offspring: And they shall spring up as among the grass, as willows by the water courses. One shall say, I am Yahuah's; and another shall call himself by the name of Jacob; and another shall subscribe with his hand unto Yahuah, and surname himself by the name of Israel. Thus saith Yahuah the King of Israel, and his redeemer Yahuah of hosts; I am the first, and I am the last; and beside me there is no Elohim. And who, as I, shall call, and shall declare it, and set it in order for me, since I appointed the ancient people? and the things that are coming, and shall come, let them shew unto them. Fear ye not, neither be afraid: have not I told thee from that time, and have declared it? ye are even my witnesses. Is there an Elohim beside me? yea, there is no Elohim; I know not any.

Isaiah 44:3-8

After Israel's release from their captivity in Egypt and uniting as a nation, the Highest lays down some ground rules in the written account of their story which are the driving force behind how others are supposed to identify this particular family of people, and what their function will be in relationship to the rest of the world for future generations to come. Having a particular group of people designated to a purpose is a pattern that can also be followed throughout Scripture and the universe. In the universe, everything has a purpose from the macro level all the way down to the micro level. These functions, some seen, others visibly unrecognizable, are all performing to allow or create balance. The Creator has used every fiber of the universe in order to tell a story. This story is to be observed in all of His handiwork; but to make the story one that everyone could understand, the Highest put His story into the only form that every human would universally experience, and that is the family. Whether good or bad, every human in order to enter this realm of existence must do so from a male and female. Functional or dysfunction this is a commonality that we all have, and this was not by mistake, but by design. The Highest chose the picture of a family and instilled all of His secrets, laws, and statutes into that family. In their proper function, they would work with Torah as an example of redemption. But, over time, through manipulation and deception, this place has been removed and forgotten by this family.

In Johann Gottlieb Fichte work titled <u>The Vocation of Man</u> (1799), He states that "you could not remove a single grain of sand from its place without thereby changing something throughout all parts of the immeasurable whole." This is the picture that we see in the cosmos when people on the planet seek out the seed of the Father, yet cannot find it because they have been moved, removed, and finally replaced. Immediately there is an imbalance that is created that affects everything.

This process of removing Yah's SEED severely affects the story that has been laid out from the beginning. The Creator designed the world to tell a story that everyone could connect with to make the world one. What has happened in recent years, due to the awakening of the "hidden ones," is now there are denial and contention about who belongs in this place. When a person brings up this necessary family, who are indispensable in humanity's redemption story, they are labeled as divisive. More importantly, those who feel this way, are a part of the strong delusion and cannot see because they choose not to. They have bought an alternative story. Truth is offensive and often hard to swallow. The great divider has always been the truth. It was never meant to divide the true believers (both blood-born and grafted), because those who are from the SEED know that there have always been different functions for all those who are in the family, but those who are not of the SEED will always perform in their function and diametrically oppose that which Yah has ordained.

In science, this truth exists and can be observed all around. In the universe there is a thing called matter and matter are made up of mostly space. This is why a person cannot walk through walls or put their hand on their desk. The reason for this is function and order. The universe is a great storyteller of how placements have a lot to do with how humanity operates on a daily basis, and atoms and matter tell it best. In exploring atoms and matter, because these substances do not evoke any emotional ties when used to testify of the precise placement of Yah's people. The reason one cannot walk through a wall is the same reason why a person cannot walk onto the field during a live soccer game. Suppose that a spot has been reserved on a community soccer field for a family, and when they get there they find another family already playing on the field with friends. Initially, they would be frustrated at the double booking of the same field, but then decide that it is not so terrible, because there is still plenty of space on the field to play. As a result, both families decides to play separate games with all the same positions on the same field (two balls and everything). Can you imagine the amount of chaos? Immediately, the other people playing would be furious. They would come over to the other family and explain how only one game can be played on the field at a time because there can only be one person for each position on the field. These are the rules. It is the same way with the table illustration in physics, and it is the same way with Yah's Chosen People on the planet.

Is there any compromise to these rules or order? Of Course! Both teams may choose to combine with what already exists and form one team and play by the rules of the game. Likewise, those who are not in the family can connect with those who are a part of the natural tree; but no matter how they chose to combine, there is one consistent rule, and that is— two of them cannot do the same thing. So, to have order in these last days, it is necessary that the children of the Highest be placed back into "play." This will then assist the rest of the world in aligning themselves with the original story of creation and order. A story of love for humanity, which can be seen through Yah choosing a people to bring order. Placing them here to bring function to dysfunction and purpose to the hopeless. This message is only carried out to completion when the natural order is not disrupted by lies and prejudice. It is Humanity's job to support Yah's Chosen. They are His Light, and when joined by their companions, humanity responds to its divine call for true harmony, order, and balance. This is the beginning of the restoration process. As the Nation of Israel is restored, the rest of the world and its elements rejoice.

[ה]

Curses & Captivity

In 1923, an anthropologist from Harvard by the name of Ronald B. Dixon wrote a book titled <u>The Racial History of Man</u>. The book sought to classify mankind into groups, not based on simply their skin color or hair, but rather to find the similarities between their physical traits and see which groups are the most closely related to others based upon skull types, place of origin, and skeletal structures. In the introduction of his work he begins to define the term "race":

> *The term "race" is one which has unfortunately acquired a somewhat different meaning in our everyday speech. We refer to the Negro of the Mongolian "race" and in so doing have in mind primarily certain general physical characteristics of color, hair,*

and features, while linguistic, cultural, historical, and political factors play but a comparatively subordinate part in our conception. We also speak, however, of the Latin, the Anglo-Saxon, or the Celtic "race," but here, although physical characteristics are in some measure concerned, it is more on language and culture, and in considerable degree on historical and political unity that our mental picture rests. From the standpoint of the anthropologist this latter use of the word "race" is inadmissible, for to him a race is a biological group based on community of physical characteristics" (Dixon, 1923).

In this passage from Ronald B. Dixon, it is easy to see the double standard placed on other "races" when trying to determine the origin of a people. In this section, I will follow the order of observational evidence. In doing so, bias will be left for logic, and cognitive dissonance will be released for the reception of truth. The Scriptures speak of not only the physical characteristics of the Hebrew people but also about the nations surrounding these people. In Biblical times race was never the issue behind contentions, it was always culture and belief (which happen to be the same thing to the Hebrew Israelite). The idea of race was never an issue in the ancient world because everyone looked relatively the same and intermingled with one another.

Dixon, in his section about the Jews, begins his dialogue about how "the racial origin of the Jews has been a fertile theme of discussion." This could be because the majority of people (including the Jewish people) had demonized the idea of being Black. While there is no real reason, one could infer that the Hebrews being any color other than that of the Anglo-Saxon would pose a serious issue for a group of people claiming to represent over 75 percent of the world's Hebrew Israelite population. Dixon goes on to write about the Jewish people stating "They were regarded as a people whose purity of blood had, in spite of wide dispersion, has been jealously preserved throughout the centuries…it appears doubtful whether… these assumptions were true…the great majority appeared to be of a different type from that found among other Semitic- speaking peoples."

The Racial History of Man goes on to not only categorize and speak about the origin of the "Jews", but also every other racial group. In doing so there are several conclusions drawn that seem to support the theory that in order to be in a particular racial class of people, especially one that was known for its region and genetic intermingling with their surrounding nations, there would have to be some evidence of their ancestral presence in their modern day appearance. What comes out is that a very significant portion of the research pointed to the Ashkenazi's of Europe (as a group), find their physical attributes directly linked to an early group called the Khazars who converted to Judaism in the Eighth Century. After researching the Jews who still had roots in other areas, there seemed to be more similarity to this group than to any other group, thus delegitimizing the claim of a pure blood line, but also leaving Professor Dixon to conclude that:

"In conclusion, if, as is probable, the Northern Arabs or Bedouin of to-day are to be regarded as the best modern representatives from the racial point of view, of the very

early Semitic-speaking peoples of whom the original Hebrews were a part, then the great majority of all the Jews today are "Semites" only in speech, and their ancestry goes back not so much to Palestine and Arabia as to the upland of Anatolia and Armenia, the caucus steppes of Central Asia, and their nearest relatives are still to be found in those areas today."

[5] *Pictures Clockwise: Northern Arab, African American (Michael Ealy), Bedouin, African American (Morris Chestnut). These pictures are used to show the similarity between the American Negro and the images provided as representatives for these groups by Dr. Ronald B. Dixon.*

Based on the information present by Ronald B. Dixon the obvious must be considered. Could it be that those who are being regarded as chosen represent another demographic of people entirely, and not because of skin color, but because of genetic and historical inconsistencies? I refrain from the argument that there are no Children of Israel who have a fair complexion or white skin, because it would be intellectually and Biblically dishonest to say that no fair-skinned person is a descendent of the scattered 10 Northern Tribes or the southern Tribe of Judah, just like it would be erroneous to believe that all Brown-skinned people are Hebrew Israelites. To draw a parallel, it must be interjected that although intermingling is a huge contention among several groups, it would be a considerable argument for such a drastic change. It is notable to mention that American Slavery does lend some validity to willful skin lightening due to "racial" mixing. One of the largest genetic evidences to a dominant group through precise genetic watering was during American Slavery. For over 400 years, the rape and prized intermingling for fairer skin and straighter hair has greatly changed the physical characteristics of a lot of slave descendants. This occurred to the point that historically America has had several presidents and well-known officials who were actually of a hybrid of "Caucasian-Negro" descent. In that time the term was called "passing," where a person through genetic washing could neglect to procreate with their own people in order to gain favor or even go unnoticed in the "dominant" society. This small truth can reiterate the fact that while the melanated people represent a large portion of the population, a person would be hard-pressed with the intermingling of the Northern Tribes, to substantiate the claim that only dark-skinned Hebrews and the forced passengers aboard slave ships are Israelites. There is more information on this topic which can be found with the passing paternal DNA and maternal DNA; and how that works, but for this section, the focus will remain simple; while skin may be fair, or the hair straight, it does not mean that these individuals lack a genetic connection to the ancestors of their Hebrew forefathers. What can be substantiated is the fact that the Southern Tribe of Judah not only stayed in the land much longer than the Northern Tribes, but also Judah has a specific set of characteristics that makes them easily identifiable. I believe that this was through the providential care of Elohim for the leaders of Israel. It should also be noted that the Tribe of Benjamin and a portion of the Tribe of Levi each had their stake with Judah.

In 70 A.D., at the time of the destruction of Jerusalem, the notable groups who were present were Benjamin, Judah, and Levi. (Due to the link of the temple with the southern kingdom of Judah it would be reasonable to note that there would be a representative from every tribe in Jerusalem or the surrounding areas during this time). It would be without robbery to reason as they migrated to escape persecution that large numbers of them stayed together. To refrain from making broad assumptions in the rest of the dialogue of locating the Chosen People, I will specifically focus on the Kingdom of Judah. This group is significant because not only are they the kingly tribe, but they are the tribe through which Yah raises up a standard for His people.

Throughout history, the Highest has always chosen a remnant of His people. The remnant would be set apart by Him in order to serve a special purpose. While each tribe of Israel had a specific purpose, it was Judah who received the role of leadership. The Tribe of Judah was not only a warrior-king tribe, but was also the leader of praise, possessing the most songs, orchestrations, and worship. Judah was also the law giver.

"The scepter shall not depart from Judah, Nor the ruler's staff from between his feet, Until Shiloh comes, And to him shall be the obedience of the peoples.

Genesis 49:10

While said characteristics can be found in other cultures, there is no other concentration of people on the planet who have this exceptionalism in praise over this tribe. It is so strong that the writings and songs from Judah are being sung all over the world, even to this day.

From the previous evidence, a person could erroneously conclude that all or only black or brown-colored skin people are the Hebrew Israelites and the chosen ones of Elohim, and that would be very far from true. What should be concluded is that the unique nature of the Hebrew people as a whole had nothing to do with their skin, as it would be almost impossible to find them just based upon skin color alone when more than a third of the world, if not more, is populated by melanated people groups. Also, that there has to be more than just the visage to make a person Hebraic.

As I transition from historical and genetic arguments to show the people, most would agree that the most compelling argument for who the Chosen People of Yah are would have to do with how their Elohim says they will be identified, because they are his and their identity and preservation are important to Him. The prophet Jeremiah spoke of a time when the Children of Israel would lose their language, culture, and their land. It is very interesting to note that out of all of the people groups on the planet there is only one historical account of a people who no one seems to know where they come from. There is only one account of a people who after serving as slaves are released and told to go return to an original continent, and not to a particular country of origin. There is only one people on the planet who believes that they grew out of the soil of the Jim Crow South or to a slave owner in one of the British colonies. There is only one group of people who Africans, Indians, Native Americans, and Arabians would hate to even be associated with. There is only one people who are scatter over the islands and the south Americas, these are the ones whom Yah Loves

But now thus saith Yahuah that created thee, O Jacob, and he that formed thee, O Israel, Fear not: for I have redeemed thee, I have called thee by thy name; thou art mine.

Isaiah 43:1

Israel was to be known by how the Highest blessed them. It was a part of their covenant relationship that as they upheld their part, that the Highest Elohim would prosper them. This prospering was not only to their benefit, but it was also to be a testimony and a witness that would draw others into the family. Now, even with a small amount of Biblical knowledge, one knows that is not what happened. Because Israel did not uphold their end of the Covenant with their Elohim, who was not merely a god, but a father to them, they had several curses placed on them. What is so magnificent about the Highest is that even though Israel did not uphold their side of the bargain He did, and even in their curses the world gets the opportunity to know who the hidden ones are. The narrative of Deuteronomy 28 starts off with this statement:

"And it will happen that if you indeed listen to the voice of Yahuah your Elohim, to diligently observe all his commandments that I am commanding you today, then Yahuah your Elohim will set you above all the nations of the earth. And all of these blessings shall come upon you, and they shall have an effect on you if you listen to the voice of Yahuah your Elohim:

For fourteen verses the Highest, through Moses, begins to tell the people of all the benefits to keeping His Commandments. In the next fifty-four verses lies the identifying markers that would be upon the Children of Israel, and why. In the section above I discussed how the whole point of prophecy was to reveal the seed inside. All of the prophecy in the Tanakh and all of the prescribed punishments to the Israelites deals with what the Highest said would come to pass because of their disobedience in Torah. All of the Biblical prophecies in the Tanakh (Old Testament) refer back to this truth and are prescribed based upon their actions in their generations. The same punishment always fits the crime, but a time came when Yah stated that they did not care about the chastisement and it was then that the fullness of their transgression brought on the fullness of his wrath.

Why should ye be stricken anymore? ye will revolt more and more: the whole head is sick, and the whole heart faint.

Isaiah 1:5

With this understanding we can see how the same things happened over and over again in the same similar manner to the Hebrews. This pattern also serves as an indication and as a foresight for the prophets of old to know what was coming. Just like a gardener, the prophet would access the fruit (Yah's children) and test the soil (the lands that surrounded or influenced them) to give the judgment that was sure to come. The prophets were sure because the Highest cannot set forth His Word and not perform it. So, in verse fifteen, Elohim tells why these things will come to pass.

"And then if you do not listen to the voice of Yahuah your Elohim by diligently observing all of his commandments and his statutes that I am commanding you today then all of these curses shall come upon you, and they shall overtake you:

Surveying the commandments written in Deuteronomy 28, Hebrew helps readers to discern that each commandment is PHYSICAL. These physical commandments would fall on a physical people. As a matter of fact, until Deuteronomy 28:46 a person can make an argument that these things could happen to anyone at any time, and that would be true. Calamity seems to befall humanity as a natural part of being in a "fallen" state, and His foresight, Elohim knows what the popular response says, so he says:

> *Moreover all these curses shall come upon thee, and shall pursue thee, and overtake thee, till thou be destroyed; because thou hearkened not unto the voice of Yahuah thy Elohim, to keep his commandments and his statutes which he commanded thee: And they shall be upon thee for a sign and for a wonder, and upon thy seed forever.*

At this moment a dialogue that could have seemingly fit all of humanity in some way, shape, or form has now been brought in with laser precision to this one particular family forever. There has been this modern movement of intellectuals and theologians who have a hard time with the word "forever." The word "forever" in verse forty-six used in this context is intriguing.

The Hebrew word for "forever" is *olam* (עולם), literally meaning to hide or a period that is beyond the field of vision of time and space. This period is a time that is either covered or unknown, and simply put, the word means "always." These curses will continue to befall on the true Children of Israel as long as they remain outside of their Covenant relationship with Yah. First, because these curses are not a one-time thing; but a process that will happen (to some degree) every time Yah's people do not obey as they have agreed to do. As a result, these people are led into captivity. Once they get out of captivity, they are not free from all future captivities, but the standard of the covenant is still in place. If these curses are true then, they should be upon whichever people claim to be this people, even today. Below, there is a list of the curse along with the verses. Read through these curses and try and find a people group that fits all of them.

Bondage, Captivity, Exile: Deut.28:41, Leviticus 26:34,36,38,41,44, Isaiah 5:13, Jeremiah 2:14, Luke 21:24

Destroyed by their enemies: Lev. 26:17, 37, Deut. 28, 25, 31, 48, 68

Exiled into the lands of their enemies: Lev.26:34,36,38,41,44

Worldwide Dispersal: Lev. 26:33, Deut. 4:27, 28:25,63, 64, 32:26, Nehemiah 1:8, Jeremiah 9:16, 13:24, 49:32

Diseases and Sickness:
Deuteronomy 28:59, 60, 61

Put lower than other groups:
Deuteronomy 28:37,43,44

Lost Identity:
Jeremiah 17:4, Psalm 83:4, Isaiah 1:3

Locked in Prisons:
Isaiah 42:22

Non-Prosperous: ("Never Do Wells"- Hilary Clinton)
Deuteronomy 28:29

An Oppressed People:
Deuteronomy 28:29, 33

Serving everyone else's gods:
Deuteronomy 28:36,64

These are the curses on the whole nation of the Hebrew Israelites, but one of the most distinct and grasping of them all is found in Deuteronomy

28:68. The verse states that they will be taken in ships and no man will buy them. It is noteworthy to mention that word "ships" is used here. It has been explained away as insignificant or as an error. Others have stated that Josephus in his Antiquity of the Jews wrote that Jews were taken by ships to Egypt to work in the salt mines and no one would hire them. There are a couple of issues with this conclusion. The first is that Egypt is walking distance from Israel, ships would not have been necessary. The next is that had he seen (or knew about) the Trans-Atlantic Slave Trade, would he have changed his mind about what being "carried off in ships" meant? During American Slavery, the people enslaved were plagued by every single curse in this chapter of Deuteronomy, down to the letter.

Below are maps to visualize what it looks like to be carried off into the four corners of the world. One map represents the Diaspora after 70A.D. from a more Eurocentric perspective, and the other is the so-called African Diaspora.

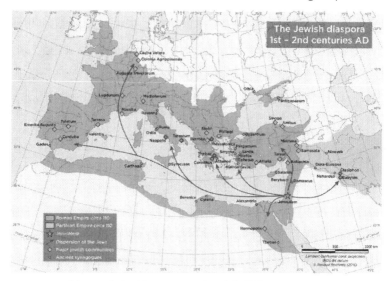

Map of the European Jewish Diaspora

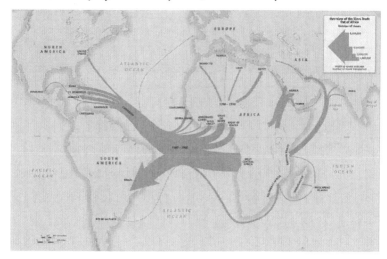

Trans-Atlantic Slave Trade Slave Dispersion

If a person would simply set aside their personal bias and look at the whole prophecy it is pretty evident who is being spoken about. The second clue can be seen in the theory of the lost tribes. Historically it has been propagated that the tribes "disappeared," leaving only the Ashkenazi Jewish population as a representation for the ancient Hebrew people. In essence, there is a book with no people; and when it comes to the so-called African-Americans who has neither their own land nor their own heritage, they are also a people with no history. Either this is an extreme coincidence or the missing people from the book and the people without a culture (who do not even know their original names) are one in the same. Many will want to turn this away as a nation of people grasping at straws to find an identity, but when Yah speaks, all others must listen and heed accordingly.

> *I thought, "I will wipe them out;*
> *I will make people forget they ever existed."*
> *If I had not feared a provocation of the enemy,*
> *lest their foes might misunderstand,*
> *lest they should say, "Our hand is*
> *triumphant, and Yahuah did not do all this."'*

For they are a nation void of sense, and there is
not any understanding in them.

If only they were wise, they would understand this;
they would discern for themselves their end.

How could one chase a thousand and two could
cause a myriad to flee, if their Rock had not sold
them, and Yahuah had not given them up? For the
fact of the matter is, their rock is not like our Rock,
and our enemies recognize this.

Deuteronomy 32:26-31

The reality is without argument. Yah has done this. Yah has removed His people. Yah has hidden them, and in these last days, this information is being brought forth to uncover those who are hidden for His Name's sake. It also means that the consequences of parents will affect the seed until a generation rises and begins to obey and keep the commandments of the Highest, thus realigning them with His blessings.

There is one key theme that sets Israel apart, and it is their captivities. While there have been many slaveries, Israel is the only nation who has had their family members (tribes) taken captive by every world "superpower." From Egypt to Rome, Israel and Judah have been slaves so often that even Yah himself had to ask the question whether not His people were just born to be slaves.

Is Israel a servant? is he a home-born slave? why is he spoiled?

Jeremiah 2:14

Egyptian Captivity

Assyrian Captivity

Babylonian Captivity

Persian Captivity

Greek Captivity

Roman Captivity

American Captivity

This marker is not just specifically slavery but the type of slavery. During the enslavement of the Hebrews, there is always the practice of trying to take away everything that makes them Hebrew. Their captors take away their names, suppress their culture, and exchange their Elohim for false gods; and this was part of the curses of Yah's people. For the captives in America, to be the people in which the Bible speaks of, this would have to be a part of their identity. Below is a brief list of "races" and their nations of origin, and not simply their continent, but their actual country.

Chinese	China
Russian	Russia
Swedish	Sweden
German	Germany
Irish	Ireland
Japanese	Japan
Nigerian	Nigeria
Egyptian	Egypt
Iranian	Iran
African-American	?????

The Negro in America has been called by every name except his or her name. No one seems to know where he or she comes from, and it is almost as if the nation popped on the scene out of nowhere. In America, Blacks seem to be a nation without conception, a nation without a home, and a nation with no Elohim of their own. They have become a nation who is void of direction and seem to be looking for anything to call their own. Even in these last days, as Judah seeks to reclaim their identity, there are constant accusations raised, that this is being done because they have nothing and no one. Scripture states that the nations will be in disbelief of who the people of the Highest are, especially in this case when we are dealing with the Royal blood line and the leader of the rest of the tribes and their companions.

But thou hast cast off, and put us to shame; And goest not forth with our armies. Thou makest us to turn back from the enemy: And they which hate us spoil for themselves. Thou hast given us like sheep appointed for meat; And hast scattered us among the heathen. Thou sellest thy people for nought, And dost not increase thy wealth by their price. Thou makest us a reproach to our neighbours, A scorn and a derision to them that are roundabout us.Thou makest us a byword among the

heathen, A shaking of the head among the people.
                                              Psalm 44:9-14

The practice of Hebrews turning a blind eye to the condition of their brother and sisters has to cease. It should not be the practice of the nations who claim to love Elohim to act as an enemy of Yah because they see the condition of His people and don't esteem nor pray for their situation. For those in disbelief, there is research to be done and a choice to be made. For those who claim to be for Yah's People, there is an obligation to the advancement of this awakening. No one will benefit as long as the identity of this People is concealed because it has always been the practice of Yah to work His plan of redemption within His home first. This entire section was written to highlight that if the Negro is the House of Judah, then there are some things that Judah should be doing, as well as there are some things that their companions should be assisting in; but with a lost identity and heritage, how do they know how to begin? The rest of this book will discuss Judah, the light that they possess, and the tasks of other nations to assist in the restoration of all of Yah's children.

[ו]

The Covenant

In the beginning the relationship between Yah and His people was discussed, along with what they mean to Him. However, merely knowing the depth of the love that the Creator has for His people is not sufficient. What has to be illuminated is what this relationship means in a Hebraic sense. The relationship between Yah and His people is a binding contract that no individual can nullify. This is not only because of His love but because of the type of contract that has been established. An ancient covenant had steps and a process that symbolized the binding effects of a Covenant between the two parties who mutually agreed to enter into the contract. Yah and His people have the same type of contract. While it is true that Yah chose His people before the foundation of the earth, it is also true that being an active part of His family and the benefits thereof require a detailed interaction between Him and His people. The Hebraic idea of a covenant is foreign to the western mind. Covenants in the Hebraic sense are binding and only voidable by the death of the other party. When it came to the Covenant with Yah and His people, it was done in this same way. Before we observe the Covenant in Scripture, we will first define what a covenant is. Just like every other term in the Hebrew language, when searched out you will find that the definition is rooted in a bio-agricultural society. The idea of a covenant is the same way. Covenant comes from the Hebrew word *barith*. Covenant is an agricultural term that deals with grain. This word originates from the Hebrew Parent Root בר. Jeff Benner in his description of *barah* states that:

"The Hebrew root ברה (BaRaH) is a child root formed out of the parent by adding the letter ה. This root has the meaning of "eat" as seen in the following verse. "And when all the people came to cause David to <u>eat</u> meat while it was yet day, David swore, saying, so do Elohim to me, and more also, if I taste bread, or ought else, till the sun be down." (2 Samuel 3:35) The noun הביר is formed by adding the letter י and has the meaning of "meat", or what is eaten. When meat was eaten by the Hebrews it was the choicest and fattest of the stock. For this reason the word BaRaH can also mean "choice" or "to choose" - "And he stood and cried unto the armies of Israel, and said unto them, Why are ye come out to set your battle in array? Am not I a Philistine, and ye servants to Saul? <u>Choose</u> you a man for you, and let him come down to me". (1 Sam 17:8).

The word *barith* carries the fullness of this meaning. The word has to do with meat, but it is often translated as covenant. In western culture trying to understand what the relationship between two parties look like can quickly die with the changing or using of words that do not convey the meaning and this word is one of those.

The word *bar* means to feed or grain. The immediate word picture deals with the bet, which is the house, and the *resh*, which is the head. The meaning in a simple form can be understood as the head of the house of the heads or head of the family. This is because at the top of the wheat and barley there are clusters that are referred to as heads which hold the seeds. These portions are where the food and the nutrition for the family come from. Also, these same heads have stalks that after releasing the heads are burned into ash that was used for soap. This soap, of course, was a cleansing agent that caused the ancients to become clean. When the letter *hey* is added to the *bet* and the rest it forms the word *barah* which is the root of the word *barith* which in English is translated as covenant. A covenant is put in place through the sacrifice of a chosen and fitting animal to be sacrificed. This was not a sick animal, or a toss-away animal. Instead, this animal was a chosen vessel that would serve as the meat to be severed or cut into two in order to allow the two parties to gather in the midst (pass through) in order to signify the bond and also the consequence for breaking it. Once the covenant was in place, just as the animals were split in two, breaking the agreement would produce the same end for the individual who broke the covenant.

In Genesis, this same exact picture took place between Yah and the forefather, Abraham:

And he said unto him, Take me an heifer of three years old, and a she goat of three years old, and a ram of three years old, and a turtledove, and a young pigeon. And he took unto him all these, and divided them in the midst, and laid each piece one against another: but the birds divided he not. And it came to pass, that, when the sun went down, and it was dark, behold a smoking furnace, and a burning lamp that passed between those pieces. In the same day Yahuah made a covenant with Abram.

Genesis 15:9-12

Therefore thus saith Yahuah; Ye have not hearkened unto me, in proclaiming liberty, everyone to his brother, and every man to his neighbor: behold, I proclaim a liberty for you, saith Yahuah, to the sword, to the pestilence, and to the famine; and I will make you to be removed into all the kingdoms of the earth. And I will give the men that have transgressed my covenant, which have not performed the words of the covenant which they had made before me, when they cut the calf in twain, and passed between the parts thereof, The princes of Judah, and the princes of Jerusalem, the eunuchs, and the priests, and all the people of the land, which passed between the parts of the calf; I will even give them into the hand of their enemies, and into the hand of them that seek their life: and their dead bodies shall be for meat unto the fowls of the heaven, and to the beasts of the earth.

Jeremiah 34:17-20

The same way the covenant was meant for the prospering and the fattening of his choice people, that same way that the covenant in Jeremiah would bring the destruction of the people. Abraham represents "head of the family, just as the top of the wheat represented that portion or substance for the rest of the family. In ancient culture seeds were not purchased in a store, they were passed down from generation to generation. The same applies with the seeds or family head of grain, the covenant that was made with Abraham was passed down throughout the family to fatten or prosper them. This covenant is binding because Yah made the covenant by Himself. He laid Abraham to sleep signifying that the Covenant was in fact binding, but that he would carry out the whole Covenant if only the people were obedient. It is a beautiful picture of being willing for service and Yah doing the rest. It is the obedience that is always better than the sacrifice. This covenant is eternal and just like the passing down of the seeds of the head from the stalk, likewise as Abraham slept, the seed in his loins that would father the physical seed of Israel was also being blessed. Spiritually, the same picture is seen in the Messiah; all who were in Him when He was obedient to the Father, are kept and upon acceptance and obedience to the call of being grafted and also heirs through His work.

Part III

The Solution

[ז]

The Foundation

If the foundations be destroyed, what can the righteous do? ~Psalm 11:3

Since the beginning of time, there has been a war for the minds of the Chosen People of Yah. Their minds have been the prime real estate for every new idea and doctrine, because every power and force knows that if the mind of the Chosen can be occupied and corrupted, then those whom they are placed in this realm to draw to the truth will follow them into destruction. It was true in the garden, and it is true now. With the rise of New Age philosophy and esoteric teachings, it seems that the foundations of the Elohim's Chosen have been shaken or even removed. The Hebrews true enlightenment has been moved out of reach through disobedience. This gift of transcendence was then discovered, coined by an outsider, and fed back to them as something new. The truth has been turned into a lie at the hands of those who look like brothers and sisters. Because their melanated pigment reflects that of the Hebrew. In rebuilding the foundation of truth, there has to be a conscious effort to reject any religion that is tied to that of previous captors. This means that practices linked to mythology, Egyptology, and all variations of the sort that are not rooted in a universal law and Torah have to be purged. Those who are ignorant of history fall into the same traps of their forefathers.

Thus saith Yahuah, learn not the way of the heathen, and be not dismayed at the signs of heaven; for the heathen are dismayed at them.

Jeremiah 10:2

While the Hebrew lifestyle is similar to other African groups, those groups should not be the authority of truth when trying to return to the covenant. Let the observational evidence speak for itself. when in reality their "truth" is the same "truth" that caused many of their ancestors to fall into idolatry and thus place them in their current situation. The other nations have constantly been a seductress to the Children of Yah. Their tactics were merely a perversion of observable evidence that was handed down through Creation to testify of Yah.

For the invisible things of him from the creation of the world are clearly seen, being understood by the things that are made, even his eternal power and Godhead; so that they are without excuse.

Romans 1:20

These nations have wowed the real Hebrews with the observable truth that was set in place to be a marker when all else fails. This New Age truth is nothing more than a Western 1970s construct that is just another ploy to take away the power and harmony of the Creator and creation, and place it in the hands of man, so the Chosen have to seek a source outside of the revealed markers in order to find enlightenment. What seems like a "new" and "deeper" understanding of the universe is only a skewed observation of the things placed here to bring the Chosen closer to their Creator. What other nations seduced Israel with was a perversion of what was already theirs. What they have discovered is a glimpse at universal foundation, and it is attractive, because it was built into the Chosen People's DNA. However, without a proper assessment of the information, and an understanding of its origin, this naivety can lead to enslavement. Complete demise and chastisement all stemming from not knowing how to handle the truth, and receiving it at the hands of another person whose intention is to control. Not being rooted in the foundations of the creator and the ancient path puts those who seek higher consciousness in bondage, and will inevitably leave them grasping for the next fleeting movement of understanding and enlightenment.

To be in debt to another for truth is exactly what Satan did to the woman in the garden. Man and woman were enlightened, and had it all, but a lower being convinced her there was more to be had. At the moment where man and woman traded their true enlightened for a counterfeit, is where the first humans go into bondage or debt, because of someone convincing them that they did not have the "true" keys to knowledge. Through a proper understanding of where the modern construct of religion comes from there can finally be a liberation of Yah's people from the bondage of religion. The separation of all falsehood can liberate Yah's people, allowing the Chosen to finally arise and regain truth and use it as intended. The Hebrew people are the light of the world, in order to see this there must be a true awakening. This awakening must be one that will assist in waking up those who are in darkness. This should not be a move into religious practices, but a call to action. The next generation must recondition and cleanse of perpetuated lies and systemic depravity. They be equipped to rule as the source of power, with the help of companions to bring harmony to a world of chaos and disorder.

Origin of Religion

For years, the so-called Black community has taken scraps from their oppressors, and pieced-together meals, with the hopes of nourishing their bodies. The same has become true with the Scriptures, which are given to Blacks in fragmented, incomplete portions as a source of pseudo nourishment for their spiritual "well-being." What many Blacks have received are the hand-me-down thoughts of so-called intellectuals, and it is with these thoughts that many of their motives and beliefs have been shaped. With the redefinition and deconstruction of the Biblical belief system by European imaginations, many have come across a watered-down, unrecognizable version of a once rich text and culture. Through the reconstruction of words and cultural practices, the eyes of many have been able to view the pages of Scripture like never before. It's through the process of observation, and repositioning of the ancient way, that many will have the opportunity to take a book that was once rejected as the "white man's" book, and for the first time, look into its pages as a mirror for the true gods of the physical realm, called Earth.

The modern concept of religion, as distinct sets of belief or doctrine, is a recent invention of the English language, and is a byproduct of colonization and globalization, in the age of European exploration, which involved contact with numerous foreign and indigenous people with non-European languages or culture.

It was primarily the dawn of major European "spiritual enlightenment" that contributed to the abstract meaning of religion. This also influenced other sacred textual definitions and their change. A system that was once viewed through a clear lens was now smudged with ink-stained hands that were in the process of rewriting history, and the understanding of Eastern culture and context, especially when it came to belief systems. It was during this period, notably the 17th Century that the word religion and the road that many would follow were paved. The base from which this change derived had no concept of this "new" construct, nor did it adequately reflect the people or the culture from which it was taken.

When a person looks up the word "religion" today, one finds a watered-down or altered abstract version of its original meaning. Like many other words or thoughts that have been handed down, this change causes confusion as well as division amongst those who are trying to find meaning and understanding in these terms. When the original idea or concept is hidden behind years of philosophy and morphological changes, it makes the journey to "truth" almost unreachable.

Definition of Religion

Religion, as it is defined today, can mean various things to different people. Religion has become a noun that describes beliefs based upon philosophy about existence, and the cause of the universe and human life. This understanding, which is purposely vague, lays the foundation that anything can be considered a religion. So much so that religion is anything that has practice, a system of behaviors, world views, sacred texts, set apart places, and societal organization. This ambiguous understanding has opened the door for what many believe is a global system of religion-A belief system based on a fleeting understanding of natural surroundings that rely on the ever-changing balance of man's emotional or societal understanding of existence. The modern understanding of religion is not religious at all, but rather an internal movement that can be eliminated and replaced as one sees fit.

Modern religion seems to find its bases in the explanation of things that individuals find mysterious because they were not there to experience. It has become the new thing to focus on things from the past instead of focusing on the things that are still available for experience and located right before one's very eyes. The only true need for going back is not to find an explanation, but instead to locate the path. Few people are serious enough about the weightier matters of divine consciousness to do what it takes to avoid the snares of man-made religious constructs and fleeting, superficial knowledge. If man would stop arguing about the origins and meanings of life and existence, and observe, humanity would find out that principles and truths are intricately woven into the very fiber of our observable environment. It is when we reach this point that a person is then able to view the physical in a deeper spiritual sense.

There are five major belief sects that have been a stronghold on the majority of the world's population. Those belief systems come from the need for the European to classify groups to control and identify them. Recently there has been the rebirth of what can be categorized as the sixth group that cyclically reappears to serve as a catalyst or comfort zone to the "conscious" community that springs up out of rebellion to the commonly accepted world systems. The sixth group is the New Age belief system that includes the Pan-African Black conscious movement. This group has wowed the masses of melanated people with its philosophy of Egyptian culture by teaching that all major religious world doctrines and principles originated with Egyptian mysticism including that of the Hebrews. While there is some validity to the origins of Egyptology in Christian practices and other groups that are offshoots of the Abrahamic faith, it is the furthest from the truth when it comes to the language and the people who existed from the beginning. The ability to be the first or have the most remaining evidence does not mean that everything that existed is the truth, or that there were no other people who had more accurate information. Take the European conquest, because of their mark on every nation. They have created a system of belief that is known and recognized throughout all the world, but it is made up of fragments of truth from other cultures, as well as a plethora of lies and paganism through mythology. If a person looked back in history and surveyed the world, because of their mass influence and support, they would believe that this was the way that it had been set up from the beginning. And just as the chosen of the Highest are finding it difficult to prove this point with the Egyptologist, the same will be true for future generations, if arguments are only from the point of dominance, rather than from the point of origin based on language and observational evidence.

The group that is dominant is always going to have the influence over what is preserved, and what is important. Historically, the Egyptians linked up with the Greeks and other European nations. It is through this allegiance that their information has been preserved, and can be seen in many Christian and subsequent religious practices. It is also a known fact that the Hebrews, during the Maccabean period fought to save their culture from being influenced by these very same people. This went as far as hiding information in caves to preserve its integrity.

Through world dominance, the Egyptian culture has influenced every nation, but it was the breaking away from this culture, and its influence that preserved the truth of the universe through the Hebrews. Being set apart in truth, was so important to the Hebrews, because they were chosen to be the keepers of truth, and the bearers of light to other nations. Egypt and other nations had their chance and steadily became a melting pot. Their observational evidence was sold and stolen through alliance with Greek nations, and likewise, when the Hebrew tried to do as the Egyptians, their information and culture met the same demise.

Man is Not Born with *His* "Religion"

He hath made everything beautiful in its time: also he hath set eternity in their heart...

Ecclesiastes 3:11a

Contrary to popular belief, man is not born with his religion but must seek it. What man is born with is his infinite self which aims to reattach to the Infinite Source from whence it originated. Eternity is bound up in the heart of man, and from an early age, the vibration and life of creation is constantly trying to draw him back to the Source. What happens is that religion, technology, and in the case of the Hebrew, discrimination, muffles this frequency. If it was not for the constant infringing of Africans existence, one could be sure that he or she would find their way back to the origin or the head of their existence. But because of the pressures of religion, humanity chooses a group often over following the Creator.

The word religion did not start out being understood as it is today. The word "religion" has experienced lots of changes over time. In Latin, religion comes from the world Religio- which means respect for what is scared, reverence for the gods, or an obligation between man and the gods. In this definition, one can immediately experience a difference between the common modern understanding of religion and the Latin definition. Cicero, who is believed to be instrumental in the origin of the word religion, defined it as Re-(again) –Lego (read). He believed that religion was to consider carefully or to go over something with the intent to reconnect. In the medieval times, religion was defined as order. What can be deduced from the old European definition of the word "religion" and the more modern interpretation is that there was still some basis of action to the word, and not just something that could be tacked on to anything that one feels is "spiritual."

In the ancient world, religion was understood as a behavior based upon observation, and never as a set of beliefs held or taught by an entity or people group who had no concrete experience with nature, or with their culture. It was never based on knowledge that had not been experienced, but on the contrary, it was based on an intuitive and unified existence with everything around them. Ancient texts (Bible, etc.) had no concept of this Anglo-European understanding of religion. It would be surprising, if read in its original language, how little, if at all, the Bible reflects modern religion, and how heavily it carries the markers of what many refer to as primitive religion. The idea of primitive religion is also a social construct, which removes the thinker away from anything that is either old or antiquated; when in reality, it is the primitive way without modern outside influences that bears the markers necessary to find the ancient path of true enlightenment and wisdom.

A Society's Law is Their Religion

All five of the major world religions: Hinduism, Judaism, Buddhism, Christianity, and Islam, were constructed by definitions, and grouped systems of beliefs that were completely foreign to the ancient people from which they originate. What is called religion today, would have been known in "ancient" times as law. There has not been, nor will there be, a society without laws.

When tackling societal laws, many people are oblivious to how much their lives are governed by their allegiance to a system. Pointing out this connection moves from being an academic share of information, to a personal endeavor to liberate a nation of people who have been hypnotically conditioned to accept their position in society without question. All previous issues culminated in where a person places their allegiances. If your allegiance is to a country or an ideology that is contrary to the Scriptural standard of obedience, then you may find yourself on the wrong side of an eternal divide. The ability for a person to be enlightened to just how much they are influenced by the rules and guidelines that surround them are imperative to the process of breaking these bonds and replacing them with the yoke of truth. Knowing the connection between how you walk and what you do can save your soul. In the book of the Revelation the mark of the beast has always been viewed with Western eyes. While it is a literal system with literal boundaries of oppression, there are also spiritual allegiances that prepare the masses to accept a physical marking in the last days. The idea that a person can simply do one thing and believe another in their heart is foreign to Yah.

If any man worship the beast and his image, and receive his mark in his forehead, or in his hand, The same shall drink of the wine of the wrath of God, which is poured out without mixture into the cup of his indignation.

Revelation 14:9-10

A teacher, by the name of Javon (Davis) Daweed, once shared with me how the future generation will be pre-conditioned by their allegiance to the Babylonian system to take the Mark of the Beast. He said the mark would first be in their spiritual hand and head before it is manifested in the physical. This is because the hand Hebraically represents what a person does and the head represents how they think. Because the laws of the system are already in the people's minds, it will eventually drive what they do. They will, without questioning, take on the physical mark of separation through societal conditioning. Just as Yah marks his chosen and sets them apart based on their allegiance to His laws, will be the same way the adversary will separate those who are choosing this system.

And Yahuah said unto him, Go through the midst of the city, through the midst of Jerusalem, and set a mark upon the foreheads of the men that sigh and that cry for all the abominations that be done in the midst thereof.

Ezekiel 9:5

"Do not harm the land or sea or trees until we have sealed the foreheads of the servants of our God."

Revelation 7:3

When Yahuah combated other nations, it was not because they did not have the law, it was because they had a perversion of the law that could be witnessed by observation and cycles of experience that did not stop at self, but returned to the infinite. Although there are similarities in the ancient culture that have to do with religious practices, these do no take away from the fact that there have been additions and subtractions from the way that man is supposed to relate to the creator. Most of these changes occurred due to a lack of understanding of how worship and obedience are embedded into creation. Mankind was never to worship creation but to use it as an avenue to understanding obedience and communion with Yah. Religion as a static ideology was never the example.

There is no Hebrew equivalent for the modern definition of "religion," because there is no support in Hebrew for a non-action based form of worship. In Hebrew, three terms deal with the word religion: *Halakh* (הלך), *Orah* (ארח), and *Dath* or *Dat* (דת). *Halakh* is the Hebrew word for walk. This is another action based word that tell how the believer has to walk the path of truth being. It literally means the way that a person lives their life. The word *Dath* or *Dat* means to "enter into the door with a mark". It can be understood as a sign of allegiance to a covenant between two parties; literally translated as law. The Hebrew word *orahh* can mean a path used by travelers as well as the path of life, a lifestyle. With this understanding, there is a concrete and functional picture, and it has nothing to do with modern religion. It would be safe to say that there is no such thing as "religion" outside of a physical walk, on a designated path, with the Creator under a covenant. Anything outside of that is a manipulation of the truth. A young scholar by the name of Troy Montaque often states that "the way of the *Hebrew* is not a religion, but a lifestyle."

When Psalm 11:3 was pinned the question had to be asked if the foundations (laws) of society are destroyed/corrupted then what will the righteous (those who depend on the order) do? If education is tainted, if government is corrupt, and if the preachers are on the payroll of the powers-that-be, how will the elect find the foundation of truth? The reality is that truth can never be hidden. The truth is around you.

---

[7] Using *Hebrew* is my own emphasis

"The heavens are telling the glory of Elohim, and the firmament proclaims the work of his hands. Every day they pour forth speech, and every night they tell knowledge. There is no speech and there are no words; their sound is inaudible. Yet in all the world their line goes out, and their words to the end of the world."

Psalm 19 1:4

The way that religion is used and conceptualized today is a modern construct that would not have had any meaning or even be understood throughout much of early history. Even now, outside of European influenced nations, people finds little functionality that can be explained outside of Western Religion. This necessity to define "religion" is a Western concern, because definition gives control and identification of various groups.

The overlapping of practices and laws was not foreign to Eastern culture. People have continually sought to place the Biblical text and the people that it speaks about into a modern religious bubble, but

Scripture and the culture of the people transcend all definitions and Western boxes.

Cultural practices that are based on observation of the material are not a religion. They are concrete experiences based upon valid evidence of function established to mirror creation and the Creator. The law of a particular place is also its religion. This can be verified by looking into all ancient and modern cultures. The law and the practices (and fulfillment of the law) are that culture or country's religion. Returning to the East. The way of the East is the way of "old." It is the path that allows us to look into the life and culture of the original people and begin to formulate our lives to reflect that life.

When a man controls the gods or the powers, it gives individuals the ability to have a monopoly on those gods. When there is one source, it takes power, and monopoly away from man, thus returning it back to the universe. The universe cannot be monopolized upon; just as there is no monopoly on a creator. No one can create light, air, or grass; and because of this, these things cannot be collectively manipulated into disobedience. Through observation, we can see that those things which are governed by a high force have stability and consistency that is not seen in man. It is this consistency that allows us to observe these evidence, and see something higher and infinite. However, with mankind, this is only done based on their interaction with the things that bear the mark of divine consistency.

Because of the foundation of law, the cycle of order, and experience being the main points of argument, we can see that it is no boasting when stating that Judah is who they are. It is merely observing a truth. Judah inherited their abilities and their identifying marks from the Creator as evidence to who these people are. If it had not been for these markers, or the fingerprint of Divine, unique abilities, and gifts, it would be impossible to identify who they are. It is the exceptionalism of the Tribe of Judah in the Americas that makes them the focal point of the world. While representing a mere 14% (or less) of the population, with more than 2/3 of those individuals either incarcerated or on drugs, it is important to mention that this particular group should not even be mentioned. In their time in the Americas, they have been some of the most active contributors to the advancement of this society. It is also important to note concerning Judah's exceptionalism, every nation which had the Children of Israel as slaves prospered, and became superpowers, thus making America and the presence of Yah's Chosen no different.

[ח]

The Source

"Whatever created the universe is sustaining the universe"-Brad Scott

Before Judah can take its rightful place amongst their people, there are a couple of prerequisites. The first is recognizing its source, and second, turning back to a pure "religion." Through slavery, the two things that were severely tainted were Judah's understanding of their Elohim and the way that they were supposed to serve Him. For the past 400 years, the Children of the Southern Kingdom have lived in a nation that has caused them to violate every one of Yah's laws. They have adopted a slave diet, worship false deities, and learned all the ways of the heathen nation that they were brought into.

> *Take heed to thyself that thou be not snared by following them, after that they be destroyed from before thee; and that thou enquire not after their gods, saying, how did these nations serve their gods? even so will I do likewise. Thou shalt not do so unto Yahuah thy Elohim: for every abomination to Yahuah, which he hateth, have they done unto their gods; for even their sons and their daughters they have burnt in the fire to their gods. What thing so ever I command you, observe to do it: thou shalt not add thereto, nor diminish from it.*

> Deuteronomy 12:28-32

As a prerequisite to reversing the curse caused by breaking the covenant, there has to be a transformation of the mindset of Yah's people while they are still in their captivity. As a people, we have to reject our slave diet and return to the diet laid out by the Heavenly Father. As a people, Judah must set aside the holidays and idols (gods of wood and stone), along with the religious systems which facilitate their worship. To do this, Judah must know who its source is, and what its original "religion" looked like.

For Judah to understand the link between them and their Creator, they must understand who He is, and why obedience is due. Many people may think through religion that they have encountered Him, but it is not until a child knows the importance of their father and all he does that they will begin to understand the honor and glory that comes with their relationship, and the same is true with Yah. For hundreds of years, there has been the effort of non-covenant parties to explain the relationship between Yah and His people. While the efforts may have sufficed, they are not conclusive and have shed very little light to the Hebrews in America on why they possess the power and the burden to gravitate to such a strong force. What man has sought to do in mythology, philosophy, and alternative religion is to explain their limited experience with the Creator and then make that a precedent for all future interaction. While man establishes a religion for control, Yahuah set up "religion" based off of His function and relation to all that is created, and anything outside is a manipulation of the truth.

Man's relation to the source is mentioned in the beginning, but the true relation with Yah and His creation, through the Biblical account, is deeper than just identifying the world's origin, which it does not seek to prove explicitly. The Biblical account of creation does not attempt to prove "how" in detail, but rather "who." This is done so that when Yah chooses a people and enforces order, it is because He knows best, and has the authority to do so.

Before any search for higher understanding of self can begin, there must be the identification of the source. There is no origin without a source. While the western mind tries to understand the origin of the source, the eastern mind seeks to understand the function of the source to align with that power and its purpose for their life. It is often through the connection or plugging into the source that we can even begin to understand why. But if man simply stands on the outside analyzing the exterior of creation yet never gets involved, then the understanding of that which it stems from will only be in form, and never function. One of the biggest lies told against the Creator is that He does not like to be questioned and that you cannot get deeper understanding. Jeremiah 29:13 says you will seek me, and find me when you seek with your whole heart. This is quite the opposite of what has been traditionally taught about the exploration of the Creator. The Creator does not want someone who is not willingly testing the limits of their faith against every source. Now, this does not mean to do as Solomon and jump off the deep end, but what it does mean is that as humans we are free to explore the function of the Creator to draw closer to Him.

The goal is not to prove the existence of the Creator. In that area, the burden of proof would be for another book, and on the person who is reading this book who believes otherwise. The sheer existence of life means that there had first to be life before that life. The life of man is the force that keeps him alive, and because force is energy, and energy cannot be destroyed only transferred, then there has to be a higher power fueling the world and keeping it from collapsing on or into itself. The purpose of deal with a source and in a broader sense this whole book is to prove and or reaffirm to Yah's Chosen people that all truth is found in Yah. Every truth, every power revealed or hidden comes from Him and is revealed through their Covenant relationship and connection.

What sets the Israelites apart from other nations is their connection with Yah and the DNA of creation through His language and His law. Torah is Yah's written guide for observational evidence and markers to reconnect with His divine being when we are separated from Him through disobedience or waywardness. Coveting what other nations portray as truth or deeper understanding is and has always been unnecessary for the Chosen. We do not need the power of multiple gods when we have the singular Elohim, and He has given us the power over all the world, the nations, and their gods. When Yah created the universe, He gave man the keys to creation. Man was immediately able to see the function of things. Adam named all the animals based upon observation and function because He understood creation. It is only through deception that the power given to man has been tainted. It was in this divine communion that man was able to unlock and explore the truth of the universe. These keys were the words of Elohim or His alephbet. In science, these are termed the letters of Creation, also known as, electrons-neutrinos, quarks, and so on—are the 'letters' of all matter." What Yah did with the universe is take the complex working of His Creation, and put them in 22 letters so that His Children would be able to understand the whole world and its function. In this language, the patterns and evidences can be observed in all of Creation. Every other nation that is outside of the Covenant relationship is only catching a glimpse of the power that Yah has given us through an intimate relationship with Him. All that is necessary to have is to be obedient and commune with Him in spirit and truth. In doing so, we function as we were ordained to in the universe and can finally stop chasing after the lower levels of truth from other nations. We have all that they have, and it is signed and guaranteed by the Creator.

Since the beginning of human existence, no one on a search for the Creator looked up into the sky and asked "what created all of this?" The question has always been "who?" What has happened over time is an atheistic evolution, or better yet devolution, of the truth of an intelligent, mindful Creator. Every culture, in their effort to reconnect with the Creator, sought to do so by making the function of that "being" personal. Where the fallacy comes into play is when the created being neglects the revealed truth of the creator and replaces it with a conceptual understanding that can be controlled. The idea of polytheism comes out of man wanting to control the forces or powers of the Creator at work in creation.

It is an ambitious task to take on trying to quantify the creator, so let's begin by stating that the Infinite is without limits, and thus, cannot be quantified by that which is finite. The question that many want to know is who the creator is? While that is a valid question, the better question is what is the Creator's function. Who is the question of form, but what is the question of function? To reach a higher level of understanding or consciousness, one must be willing to let go of the mind of the oppressor, and his system. Looking through an abstract lens that has been given and perpetuated by Europeans has no place in the understanding of deeper matters. It is the way of the ancestors that allows us to unlock the path to knowledge. It is the Eastern (*qedem*) way that affords us a glimpse into the infinite that would otherwise be off limits to our spectrum of view (we will deal with that later).

Before there was the manifestation of Yah, there was that which was immaterial or unseen without the proper measurements necessary in this realm known as Earth. Before there was any beholding, there was the Infinite Limitless Creator. In the Hebrew Bible, this Creator is viewed in the masculine. This is done because there is no gender neutral in Hebrew. It is either masculine or feminine in understanding and function. While we are acutely aware that the Infinite One is not bound by gender or man's finite understanding, it is through the progressive and full understanding of Scriptures that we know that the Infinite One would eventually choose a form in which to reveal that essence that cannot be understood outside of our limited realm.

The reality of the Infinite One is that there cannot be boundaries set to define the real creative genius of the universe. To set those bounds places the creation instantly in idolatry by separating and limiting the power of the Creator. The harmony of the forces sent forth for creation through the Infinite is one. Everything is part of a greater whole, yet only the source from which the created comes from should be worshiped. [The creative powers *avod* (serve) the one from which they originate.] We are to serve the fullness of the majesty of the Infinite, rather than just the finite parts that we can understand or identify with. It is the function of humans only to identify with those who share the same form as they do, which immediately negates and destroys the genius of diversity that was placed here by the Creator. Our diversity in physical visage and spiritual function are all key pieces to a much larger puzzle. It has been said that it is hard for people to identify with something when they believe that they are not included in the plan. And because of this, it has been the plan of man to suppress the truth, because they believe that their role is not significant. This cannot be further from the truth when it comes to the Highest's plan for humanity. His function is unity and harmony, and just because a person does not see why this won't change the function that has been set forth. Manipulating the order or the variables will not bring harmony, only chaos. So, what Yah is doing is using His Chosen to reveal His Function, thus renting the veil from the Earth to behold His majesty.

In Hebrew, there are things that are *Qoph* or beyond your realm of understanding by relating to the physical things that are around you. Each person can see Yah. It is through His people that His truth is revealed. Every book of The Bible and every word that is brought forth comes from a person, that has committed to the truth of the revealed function of Yah and His people and sought to bring it forth for the revelation and gathering of His people. In these current times, there are still things that are not seen based upon a limited spectrum of vision caused by systematic mass confusion, and the distortion of the frequency sent forth into the universe by the creator in the form and function of a Chosen People. Even with a Chosen People and those things around us we do not fully understand the Creator because creation is finite in how we experience it based upon our personal biases and unwillingness to embrace all of our function as a collective unit. It will not be until we see our Yah as the one who is only tangible through a relationship with his people that we will cease manipulating his function to propagate a personal agenda to nullify the importance of our role and those around us. The revelation of Judah makes the creator identifiable by his creation at a time where he seems far off and distant at the time of such calamity. So by understanding the function of his people in the universe and who they are gives each person the opportunity to unveil the hidden parts of Yah to see Him and His plan for humanity clearly.

The Strong Binder of Creation

Who is this one that is the strong binder through the known world? Is it a personal god that has traveled through other cultures, or is it a high power that has stood the test of time, and has ownership over the created but is not manipulated or sustained by that which it has sent forth. The infinite is not dependent on the finite but vice versa. Elohim understood through the eyes of religion and European form, makes Elohim need man while Elohim is not understood in His infinite sense as dependent on any force that is itself dependent. Elohim is not merely the Creator of the universe, as His dynamic presence is necessary to sustain the existence of every created thing, small and great, visible and invisible. That is, Elohim's energies (operations) maintain the existence of the created order, and all created beings, even if those agencies have explicitly rejected him. It lies in understanding how great his plan is, and how small we are that we can begin to align ourselves with the greater mission. The sheer fact that we are allowed to be a vehicle in any way to a creator like this should compel the chosen to step into their rightful place, and for their companions who are also chosen, and called out to gather together in order to be used for His glory.

Man cannot take on the function of Yah

The Infinite is what scientist refer to as nucleic bonding or the strong force. These elements are recognized as gravity and electromagnetism, and they simply exist. If it weren't for this bonding and a constant input of energy by the source, then as stated in the second law of thermodynamics, unless new energy is introduced over time, then all systems would deteriorate. This law confirms that without an Infinite Source of power that is attached and working in the creation, the world that we know would return into a primordial chaotic state. This basic understanding takes power out of the hands of any created being or entity and places it outside of a finite understanding. No man who deteriorates and returns to the dust, from which he came, can claim to be adding back the necessary power to sustain a universe. This power is beyond mortal "god" power. It's larger and more infinite.

[ט]

The Messiah

The visible universe is made up things that cannot be seen, unless, they are revealed. Many people outside of special circumstances have decent vision. When a person can physically see, and experience the world, there are still limitations. There are things which must be explained to illuminate a person's vision past what can be seen on the surface. This applies to our physical world, and also the spiritual world, which, believe it or not, work hand and hand to reveal the truth.

In the physical world, man has sought to explain the unseen through science. While some science is nothing more than empty rhetoric, there is other information from observational evidence that can lend deeper meaning to complex concepts.

Albert Einstein is famously known for his equation of $E=mc^2$[8], which shows that the increased relativistic mass (m) of a body comes from the energy of motion of the body—that is, its kinetic energy (E)—divided by the speed of light squared (c^2). This equation expresses the fact that mass and energy are the same physical entity, and can be changed into each other.

In the beginning was the Word, and the Word was with Elohim, and the Word was Elohim. This one was in the beginning with Elohim. All things came into being through him, and apart from him not one thing came into being that has come into being. In him was life, and the life was the light of humanity. And the light shines in the darkness, and the darkness did not overcome it. The true light, who gives light to every person, was coming into the world. He was in the world, and the world came into being through him, and the world did not recognize him. He came to his own things, and his own people did not receive him.

John 1:1-5,9-11

---

[8] https://www.britannica.com/science/E-mc2-equation

Who, being in the form of Elohim, thought it not robbery to be equal with Elohim:

Philippians 2:6

I and my Father are one.

John 10:30

who is the image of the invisible Elohim, the firstborn over all creation, because all things in the heavens and on the earth were created by him, things visible and things invisible, whether thrones or dominions or rulers or powers, all things were created through him and for him, and he himself is before all things, and in him all things are held together,

Colossians 1:15-17

Every object that we can physically engage with our senses is made up of atoms. This ordinary atomic matter (stuff) is floating around separate, unable to be seen or interacted with. An atom is the smallest part of an element that contains all the properties of that element. Anything smaller than an atom is a subatomic particle. This is obviously more complicated, but with a comparison of this information to Torah, and what can be observed in its relationship to the universe, it makes good sense. In observing the effects of atoms, we know that 99.9999999999999% of the content of that atom are unseen. That unseen element is not nonexistent but is force or energy. The 99.9999999999999% you cannot see is much greater than the minuscule percentage of what you can see. But it is not until those unseen elements are acted upon by a very strong invisible force that those things which were hidden, then become visible, and operate with a purpose. The reason why Yah choose to reveal Himself is because He does not wish to remain hidden. The reason why He chooses vehicles to manifest His power is because He wants to show His people the concealed parts of Himself. It is not until we begin to mirror His word that we can see Him because it is through His word that He is made visible. We are starting to see the Father when we become one with the visible testimony of His power. This is why it is important never to want to downplay either side, spiritual (unseen) or physical (what is manifest) because both elements work together to produce what is experienced as reality. Taking away any part would then be destruction and chaos.

But it is easier for heaven and earth to pass away than for a single stroke of a pen to drop out of the Law.

Luke 16:17

The works of his hands are verity and judgment; all his commandments are sure. They stand fast for ever and ever, and are done in truth and uprightness. He sent redemption unto his people: he hath commanded his covenant forever: holy and reverend is his name.

Psalm 111:7-9

Everything that we experience is based upon the energy or power of the Creator converted into matter. This visibility gives the immediate opportunity to connect with our creator, as well as to see and understand him based upon the elements of creation. While the creation clearly testifies, the Highest did not see it fit to stop there, but goes a step further to speak on his own behalf in a form that all those who walk on the earth can recognize and relate. Because of religion, many people have distorted this picture and caused the chosen of Yah to reject their Messiah. In doing so, there is a void, and a missing key that sheds light and truth on the current situation of the Hebrew, as well as the remedy. In the Messiah due, to not understanding the observational evidence, many also run the risk of denying their very place in the world as his elect.

Vision in itself is a magnificent thing, but what is interesting about vision, is even with 20/20 vision, humanity is only seeing a small fraction of what is actually visible. Based upon the light that the physical eye can receive, humanity is seeing only .035% of what is actually visible, and the other 99.9965% of the visible universe remains concealed in plain sight.

Visible light is the light that we can see, and thus is the only light detectable by the human eye. White light is visible light, and it contains all the colors of the rainbow, from red to violet. With this understanding of the unseen world, it is more than safe to say that the way that things are perceived on the surface must be evaluated deeper than what has been popularly considered in many religious circles. Our eyes are not the only way that we see, and it serves to reason that we must be illuminated or enlightened beyond the small spectrum of white light in order to unlock the deeper insights of the universe.

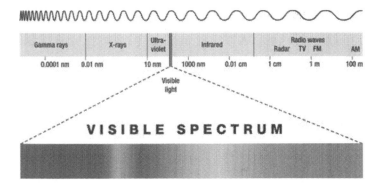

The Keys are found on earth as they are in heaven. The visible keys are a mirror to that which cannot be seen. These unseen elements are equal to the seen elements. The unseen is very real and very powerful. This can be proven based upon how much is manifested in a very small visible reality. It is theorized that more than 99.9999999999999%

of what we encounter atomically is unseen, leaving only 0.0000000000001% which is visible. The invisible percent can be described as energy or force, and the visible percentage is the manifestation of the larger unseen force. In this realm, we as the Children of Israel are the seen force (0.0000000000001%) through which the greater unseen force (99.9999999999999%) chooses to manifest His power. This is not implying Yah is merely energy, but rather power, and all that power in its infinite forms and sources are accessible to us through Yah.

If this is true for man, then it must also be true for Messiah and much more. Messiah is the 0.000000001% of the unseen as well. He represents the portion of Yah's word that manifest as an example, as well as the hidden parts of the Israelite that can only be seen through obedience, thus, becoming the ultimate vehicle through which the power of Yah is manifested.

Before we get into arguments about what can't be seen, let's look at this through a logical observational lens. What is harder, the 99.9999999999999% of unseen existing, or that power manifesting itself in a physical 0.00000000001% form? You be the judge.

The idea of being non-Messianic is foreign to Scriptures. Not agreeing on the time of Messiah, or even his revelation is one thing, but labeling oneself as non-Messianic and Hebrew Israelite is an oxymoron. By nature, and as a part of your national conception, you are Messianic. מח (*mach*) is the two letter root of the word Messiah, which means to strike or marrow[9]. This comes from the *mem*, which is water, and the *het,* which is the wall. The combined meaning is liquid that is separated or inside. In order to obtain the substance or fat inside the wall (or bone), the outer portion must be broken or afflicted. Just as the alabaster box of Mariam Magdalene was pouring out after being broken to anoint Messiah, the same way that Yah has broken the Children of Israel, so that the sweet savor of their prayers can raise up and reach the father. The term Messiah comes from the Hebrew root word mashach (משח). The word means

---

9 a soft fatty substance in the cavities of bones, in which blood cells are produced

separated out, but is commonly translated as anointed. The anointed one is the person who has been separated out to an office of authority (prophet, priest, or king) by being smeared with oil for the work of Yah. This person was also a brother of the people. In the Hebrew language a brother is an *ach* (אח). It serves to mention that any messiah that is not the brother of the Hebrew people, is not the anointed one.

> *Thou shalt in any wise set him king over thee, whom the LORD thy God shall choose: one from among thy brethren shalt thou set king over thee: thou mayest not set a stranger over thee, which is not thy brother.*

> Deuteronomy 15:15

The one Yah chooses will be the one anointed and drawn out for His glory. The Messiah will not be one who is drawn out for his own glory, but He is set apart to also draw out others.

Father, glorify thy name. Then came there a voice from heaven, saying, I have both glorified it, and will glorify it again.

John 12:28

Let your light so shine before men, that they may see your good works, and glorify your Father which is in heaven.

Matthew 5:16

The physical Messiah is not just a person, but also a cyclical pattern of operation that can be observed throughout Scriptures, and is placed in each one of us. The idea throughout Biblical history and even modern history is that there have been individuals who have risen up as liberators and leaders of nations is not something foreign to Scripture. It is stated in the *Brit Chadasha* (New Testament) that many "messiahs" will come in his name.

I am come in my Father's name, and ye receive me not: if another shall come in his own name, him ye will receive.

John 5:43

For many will come in My name, saying, I am the Messiah,' and they will deceive many.

Matthew 24:5

This idea of multiple "messiahs" is both literal and spiritual. The name being the character or the spirit of a savior, yet many have no power to enforce or fulfill the purpose of Torah. Many people today follow a lot of false Messiah's. Some see themselves as such, yet have not embraced the picture that is being set forth that must be coupled with the laws, statutes, and commandments to manifest the change that is being sought. The picture that is being presented is one that represents the cyclical pattern of redemption, as well as the picture that can be paralleled to Hebrew who is in the land of their captivity today. Because the Messiah is attached to the people of Judah and the Israelites as a whole, many similarities can be perceived by himself and his family: both past and present. Similar to the so-called Negro the Messiah was oppressed. The Messiah played music and danced in his physical poverty. He lived in a land

Like Today's Black people

where the rulers over him wanted him dead. He lived in a land where he was displaced by the powers-that-be, to hide his family and his true identity. He lived in a land where the positions were reversed. The servant was in his house, while he didn't even have a place to lay his head. He was likened to the lowest in society. The powers of the time even said that the Messiah was not of the royal blood that he claimed, but that he lied about his father and his true heritage. They also went as far as to say that nothing good could come of him, because of where he was born. They plotted out and killed him although he was innocent and then after he was dead said he was still a threat. All of these parallels and more can be seen in his family today. The same man also became all the curses for his people, yet in his obedience was able to break the bonds of generational curses for the illumination of the SEED of Abraham through his testimony. The picture of the Messiah is supposed to constantly bring humanity back to the original picture of a relationship that is bound by the obedience and blessing of Yahuah. The Messiah comes in the character of the Father, to point out salvation, to bring the world back to the picture of the family, and what salvation means without religious dogma and falsehoods. Messiah is the way. The Messiah shows the order that Yah has outlined in him as the cornerstone; Giving the world a reference point for its savior. By acting as the visible image of the unseen Elohim, Yahusha shows that resurrection, life, and rescue come from obedience to the Father, and by being the reflection of his word. He reveals that Yah is who saves the family (the seed, the בֵּן (son))

I, even I, am Yahuah; and beside me there is no saviour.

Isaiah 43:11

For thy Maker is thine husband; Yahuah of hosts is his name; and thy Redeemer the Holy One of Israel; The Elohim of the whole earth shall he be called.

Isaiah 54:5

Just as no one can save you but Yah, another cannot come along offering an alternative to getting from out of his curses. "Jesus" cannot sacrifice for man to be out of bondage because obedience is better than sacrifice (1 Sam. 15:22). It was not the sacrifice that held power, but the obedience of the one that was being afflicted likewise. It does not matter if we trust in the sacrifice, and do not match our faith with obedience. If you believed, you would do.

"For if you had believed Moses, you would believe me, for that one wrote about me. But if you do not believe that one's writings, how will you believe my words?"

John 5:46-47

An action based language must be visible through observational evidence. The Hebrew language is function before it is form. Through the "Old Testament," we see the function of the Word of Yah. In Messiah, we see the form (the visible image of the unseen) manifest in the flesh to give working definitions of what it looked like to live out Torah. For the so-called Negro in America, the picture of the Messiah should have been familiar.

It is my strong belief that the salvation that was wrought on the cross (tree) was for His Chosen People and their companions. This was not meant to be interpreted as a way to get out from under the family and its rules, but rather a testament to how tight we should cling to them, to show evidence of our relationship with the Father. The Christian Eurocentric version of that picture paints a universal idea that is foreign to Scriptures. When the Scriptures says that Yah so loved the world, it should say that Yah so loved his chosen that had been scattered throughout the world. Those who are a part of His set apart family.

I love them that love me; and those that seek me early shall find me.

Proverbs 8:17

Now then, if you will indeed obey My voice and keep My covenant, then you shall be My own possession among all the peoples, for all the earth is Mine;

Exodus 19:5

And all the inhabitants of the earth are reputed as nothing: and he doeth according to his will in the army of heaven, and among the inhabitants of the earth: and none can stay his hand, or say unto him, What doest thou?

Daniel 4:35

"I have loved you," says Yahuah. But you say, "How have You loved us?" "Was not Esau Jacob's brother?" declares Yahuah. "Yet I have loved Jacob;

Malachi 1:2

The Messiah coming was Grace and Mercy. How the Messiah was treated, and his death was a foreshadowing of the treatment of the Israelites in their last captivity in every corner of the earth, especially in the Americas. When the Children of Elohim in the Americas were brought here on slave ships and mistreated they were supposed to remember the words of their ancestors, but due to the erasing and removal of everything cultural that became a difficulty over time. When the Children of Israel were taken into their final captivity and spoon fed their Scriptures, one part should have seemed all too familiar. The story of a man (even if the image[10] had been changed to portray a European) who was despised, mistreated, tortured, whipped, and beaten was supposed to remind them of themselves. They were expected to see his life, death, burial, and resurrection, and be compelled to ask how did he receive new life.

In their observation, they were supposed to see his obedience to Yah and immediately follow him for YAH to turn their captivity.

"After two days will he revive us: in the third day he will raise us up, and we shall live in his sight."

Hosea 6:2

But the Adversary being crafty and cunning implemented a diversion through mass religious mind control, and what transpired is the Eurocentric Christian model of salvation through stagnant belief. An intellectual faith was born. The

---

[10] Cesare Borgia

idea that a person could simply think something was true and that concept became what people believed as "salvation". The European told the slave to believe in Jesus to be saved, rather than to follow him to the Father to follow Torah. This same lie was passed down and tainted the original picture of the gospel, which was to compel the reader to a life of obedience to the laws, statutes, and commandments of Yah as a witness to this inward conversion.

For close to 400 years, the people in this nation have bought this lie of belief without action, hook, line, and sinker. When the whole Bible talks about the people returning to Yah, it never once says in Torah that Yah's salvation is a wild card that trumps His instructions. It is the obedience to His teaching that brings about salvation. The Messiah showed this by being obedient until the end, thus being resurrected or "saved." There is no way for us to get around keeping the commandments of Yah. The Messiah did not come to die for our sins. Every man must die for his own sins. The job of Messiah was to be a physical representation of Torah, and how the word does not change, and obedience to Yah is our salvation. Scripture teaches that we are to work out our salvation. We have to live it out. What has been done in the Messiah is the ability to see our redemption and the process that has been set forth. We are supposed to see a mirror image of ourselves, and his life and obedience are to compel us to the Father.

Since only the Father can save His people, He does so with the only thing that has come forth from Him that does not change, and that is His Word. It is His Word which brings blessings and the curses. Thus it can only be by the decree of His Word, and the promise not to forsake His people that brought salvation. The Word of the Highest and who He is are one. When His Word goes forth, he has also gone to perform it. If His Word brings salvation and turns the captivities of His people, then he has done so. The Word is the SEED, and the SEED has the life within it. The SEED is tried, and is resurrected. If His people have this same SEED in them, through the promise to Abraham, then that same resurrection is in each of them only waiting to be brought back to life through obedience to the covenant of the family.

When Israel failed to carry out their role as a collective nation, Yah didn't negate the nation, but instead he raises up ONE who will show the power the people were supposed to manifest, had they connected to the source without restriction.

Verily, verily, I say unto you, He that believeth on me, the works that I do shall he do also; and greater works than these shall he do; because I go unto my Father.

John 14:2

In the beginning of this book, the covenant and the ancient Hebrew people, as they relate to Yah was discussed. It is common knowledge that the Messiah would be a kinsman to his people. In order to be the Messiah, Yahusha must also carry the same curses of the Hebrew people.

Christ hath redeemed us from the curse of the law, being made a curse for us: for it is written, Cursed is every one that hangeth on a tree:

Galatians 3:13

By doing so, this allows us to see a mirror image of our affliction. The world hated the Messiah, and He told his followers that the world would hate them, also. Even when He did the right thing, it was seen as wicked. He was in bondage within his land because the Romans had placed their own religious and kingship in place. At the time of the Messiah, Yahushua is supposed to be King, and John the Baptist (Yahacanon) is supposed to be high priest, yet someone else was on the throne. Immediately, you saw the picture of Judah (in Messiah) as the light of the world in the midst of a broken society and viewed as a poor young man. He has a mother who supposedly is a disgrace to her family for becoming a mother before she completed her covenant with her groom (baby out of wedlock). This picture is all too familiar for many Blacks in America. The power of Messiah drew people to Him. He was the talk of Jerusalem. It was a love to hate kind of situation. On the one hand, the people loved him. On the other, the religious elite feared the change that would come if he woke the people up to the game that was being played on them. Likewise, that is the same function of Hebrews today in the midst of an oppressive system. Hebrews are supposed to take on the spirit of the Messiah and wake up people to their true identity and purpose. Time has come to cease contemplating how an emancipation from a system established in opposition to Yah's laws will affect those who built the system. Considering life over obedience removes the ability to be counted worthy. The example of the Messiah shows how the world will behold his chosen, know who they are, but reject them.

> *He was in the world, and the world was made by him, and the world knew him not.*
>
> John 1:10

This is why in the last days, just as in the time of Messiah, he had to make it known through the testimony of the saints that the person (people) who the world despises are mine.

> *Behold, I will make them of the synagogue of Satan, which say they are Jews, and are not, but do lie;*

behold, I will make them to come and worship before
thy feet, and to know that I have loved thee.

Revelation 3:9

They hate the light. One of the most interesting
lines about the identity of the Messiah gives us the
clue to the knowledge of the religious elite and that
is when Nicodemus came to the Messiah. He told
him that they knew who he was, because of what
he had done.

"Now there was a man of the Pharisees whose name
was Nicodemus, a ruler of the Jews. ²This man came
to him at night and said to him, "Rabbi, we know
that you are a teacher who has come from Elohim,
for no one is able to perform these signs that you are
performing unless Elohim were with him."

John 3:1-2

The same goes for Hebrews today. As they begin to
follow in our rightful place, the knowledge of who
they are will be progressively made to manifest.
Also, powers-that-be are exposed by the revelation

of the truth they and their forefathers have tried to suppress through years of systemic racism and oppression. The very truth that was concealed from the masses regarding the identity of the chosen ones that are in the belly of the beast here in the United States of America. This is the time of the manifestations of the sons of Yah. Just as the crucifixion (hanging on a tree of Messiah) drew the whole world's attention to the Messiah, in like manner Jacob's Trouble will bring the whole world's attention to the true chosen of Yah. The world is witnessing it happen before their eyes, as the whole world is brought to a central focus. The killings of blacks in America, even in their rugged and oppressed condition is a topic which has become famous all over the world. Affliction must also be coupled with a testament of obedience. If the adversary can continue to bring accusations to the Father, against His children for breaking his commandments, he will continually be allowed to afflict them as the prince of this realm. It is the knowledge of their function that should give the power that is needed to raise up as an ensign to the nations.

[י]

The Companion

And one shall say unto him, what are these wounds in thine hands? Then he shall answer, those with which I was wounded in the house of my friends. Zech. 13:6

After reading the evidence and knowing who the Hebrews are it may now be asked, "So, now what?" You agree that there is a connection between yourself and the children of the Bible or you know that you have identified the wrong people as the Jews. If you are in either position the response to both has to be repentance. The necessity of repentance after coming to the knowledge of truth is imperative. For the Hebrew, it is important to rejoin into Covenant. Likewise, it is equally important for the companion. But what makes the position of the companion more critical is because there is a double negative. There is not only the issue of being outside of Covenant, but there is the added issue of the blood of the children of Elohim on your hands. The same way the curses have followed the Hebrews in America and abroad is the same way that the atrocities of the American ancestors have followed them. This is not limited to just Whites, but the individuals whether fellow Hebrew (i.e. Arabs and Egyptian-Hebrews through the wives of Abraham and Ishmael), or Kemetic (Hamite) nations who participated in the selling, transporting, and conspiring of Yah's people. Each group who had a hand in the atrocities tied to the crafty counsel have to turn and repent. Those who were supposed to be friends to the Israelites have failed and have caused trouble. The things that have happened to the Israelites in America and the bloodshed is also on your hands. Being faced with this reality is the first step to mending the relationship of unity that was supposed to come as a result of a cooperative relationship with Yah's Chosen people. Have you blessed or cursed yourself with your actions against Yah's Chosen people?

And I will bless them that bless thee, and curse him that curseth thee: and in thee shall all families of the earth be blessed.

Genesis 12:3

The nations are also under a curse. If you have participated in cursing the seed of Abraham, then you will also partake of the curses that come with this particular action.

"Our present condition needs serious recognition"

~ Ms. Lauryn Hill

Many ask why it matters if the nations recognize who the Hebrews are? For all intents and purposes one could argue that as long as the Hebrews know then, there should not be any further concern. The situation is deeper than mere knowledge of self. It matters because their role as a part of the whole is imperative to their companion's redemption. As a Hebrew awaiting redemption, I see two things shortly; the first is the restoration of my people, and the other is the recompense for the actions against the apple of Yah's eye. Making a choice is an active response to which side of Yah's wrath people will be on.

Ho, ho, come forth, and flee from the land of the north, saith Yahuah: for I have spread you abroad as the four winds of the heaven, saith Yahuah. Deliver thyself, O Zion, that dwellest with the daughter of Babylon. For thus saith Yahuah of hosts; After the glory hath he sent me unto the nations which spoiled you: for he that toucheth you toucheth the apple of his eye.

Zechariah 2:6-8

Hebrews being outside of their position is their problem because of their disobedience, but the treatment they have experienced in America (because of a misunderstanding of their "low position") is an entirely different situation. Knowing who they are and knowing what the companion's role entails, as a family member (blood-born or grafted), can directly affect their position in the Kingdom as well-being situated on the wrong side of the Father's wrath. Now, many still may feel like they are not in a contrary position based on a personal assessment of "wrongs," but the reality is that the atrocities of slavery and racism still exist, and drive interactions between other nations and the Hebrew descendants in America. The acts and ideologies set forth to destroy the seed still exist, they are currently functioning under a different guise. Slavery, due to the crafty wording of the 13th Amendment and taskmasters (police), still exist just under a different visage. The Hebrews in America are still being wounded in the house of those who claim to be their "companions" because of their belief in their "Elohim," and many of them are staying silent to be politically correct. If a person's family member kills a loved one of another and then dies without being convicted, it is a tragedy without measure? But imagine if later that the person has to forgive the killer of her loved one, yet they continually stand before them with the blood of the slain on their garment, it makes it hard to forgive them, even if they have not exhibited any of the behaviors of their ancestors.

Are the other nations responsible for the welfare of Yah's Chosen People? Does this only happen once they decide to join the family? Will the Nations be held accountable for what has taken place in their midst? Or is everyone now allowed to operate in the spirit of Cain?

"And Yahuah said unto Cain, where is Abel thy brother? And he said, I know not: Am I my brother's keeper? And he said, what hast thou done? The voice of thy brother's blood crieth unto me from the ground. And

now art thou cursed from the earth, which hath opened her mouth to receive thy brother's blood from thy hand"

Genesis 4:9-11

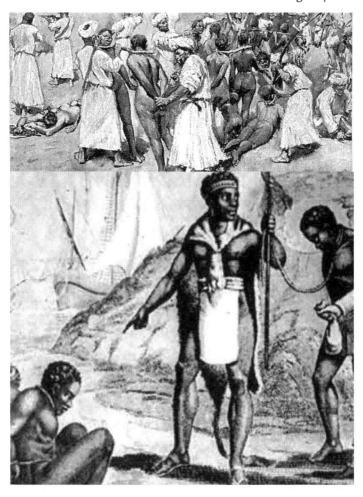

***The images depicted are of native Africans and Arab slave traders who were instrumental in the selling of the Hebrews into Slavery. The ones proceeding these are to show the treatment of the so-called Negro, and what they were subject to because of their disobedience and the cyclical process of slavery (for more on this topic, please see the section Redemption). The nature of these images is not to be contentious, but instead to point out how all parties (including the Hebrews) are collectively responsible for the condition of the Hebrews in captivity. All nations (depicted or Historically implied) participated whether directly or indirectly to the current predicament and continual mistreatment of Yah's Children; which includes but is not limited to their treatment in American Captivity, even until this present day.

AN ARAB SLAVE MASTER.

Slaves chained and yoked like cattle

Slaves ship siege after illegal transport

O daughter of Babylon, you devastated one, how blessed will be the one who repays you with the recompense with which you have repaid us.

Psalm 137:8

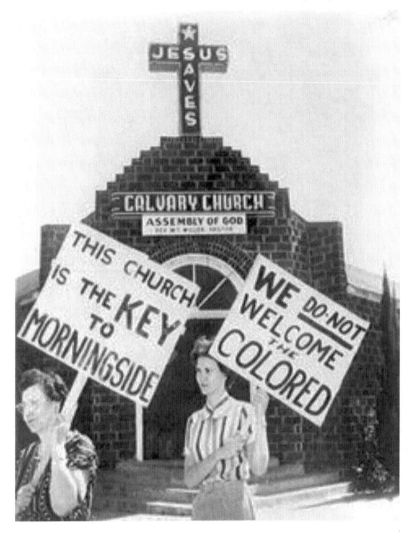

They have also surrounded me with words of hatred, and
fought against me without cause.

Psalm 109:3

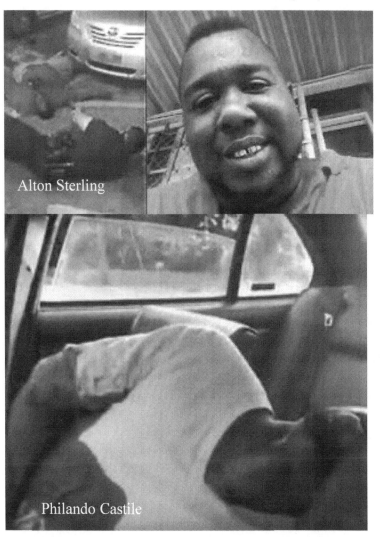

Alton Sterling

Philando Castile

And their bows will mow down the young men, they will not even have compassion on the fruit of the womb, Nor will their eye pity children.

Isaiah 13:18

"Therefore her young men will fall in her streets, and all her men of war will be silenced in that day," declares Yahuah.

Jeremiah 50:30

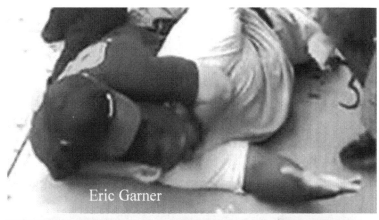

Eric Garner

YOU ARE KILLING US

Whose possessors slay them, and hold themselves not guilty: and they that sell them say, Blessed be Yahuah; for I am rich: and their own shepherds pity them not.

Zechariah 11:5

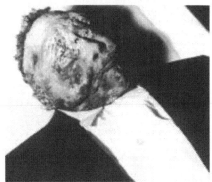

Emmet Till

Hazael said, "Why does my lord weep?" Then he answered, "Because I know the evil that you will do to the sons of Israel: their strongholds you will set on fire, and their young men you will kill with the sword, and their little ones you will dash in pieces, and their women with child you will rip up."

2 Kings 8:12

Yet she became an exile, she went into captivity; Also her small children were dashed to pieces At the head of every street; They cast lots for her honorable men, And all her great men were bound with fetters.

Nahum 3:10

Close-up of the lynching
(Georgia Department of Archives)

*And I am very sore displeased with the heathen that are at
ease: for I was but a little displeased, and they helped
forward the affliction.*

Zechariah 1:15

Seeing His people and not calling on the Father on their behalf is unacceptable. To stand and watch innocent killings and not become a part of the solution is unacceptable. If you see a child of the Father wounded and did not say anything, then you are just as guilty as the one who wounded them. To look upon the wound of slavery and oppression that the Israelites in America bear and to encourage, neglect their cries, or tell them to remain silent is not only hateful but also the highest level of anti-Semitism.

Without repentance there can be no remission
-Ms. Lauryn Hill

As a person on the "inside", I know first-hand of the pain caused by the affliction of Yah's Chosen, and I also know the control that is given to the adversary when we neglect to put into action what we know is right to remedy these curses. As a people, we are more than aware what our purpose is by now, but we still want to walk in that purpose carrying baggage. In order advance, there are necessary steps to taken on both sides of history. Whether we have been the victimizer or the victim, there is a way to stop these cycles of abuse. It's not an individual task, but a joint effort.

If we must repent before we can return into Covenant with Yah, then our companions must repent before they can come into covenant with us. A covenant is built on mutual trust and upholding the tenants of the agreement above all else. It is important that the companion finds safety in the House of the Father, but how can both the People and the companion dwell in the same place when they have the blood from the sins of your forefathers upon you? Many White people in America and other nations around the world are claiming to be in the House of the Father, yet they are trying to enter with soiled garments. Can you imagine entering the house of the father whose children your forefathers killed wearing passed-down clothes with the blood stains fresh upon them? It would be hard for the person not to see you as a reflection of the person that caused their family so much pain. The companion must take off the garment of their family. In Torah, it was the practice of the Hebrews when they took a wife from the spoils of war to cut her hair and her nails and allow her to mourn her family before she was brought into covenant with her husband and new family. I submit that the same is necessary for the Gentile seeking to be grafted into the family after the tragedies of American Slavery and the genocide of Israelites in the Americas, the islands, and beyond. The remedy is to come into covenant, to avoid having the vengeance of the Kinsman Redeemer enacted upon you, there must be cutting off of all that is connected to foreign heritage, and culture in opposition to the plan of the creator of the universe. American pride and identity cannot be found amongst the companion of Judah and Ephraim. To be one, the two cannot identify different culturally. The garment of White supremacy and oppression has to come off.

It is a denial of self. Messiah, as the ultimate representative of the Hebrew family, makes this claim to His followers. As the Israelites begin to walk in obedience and return to the Laws, Statues, and Commandments of their Elohim, they will suffer a refining process through persecution known as Jacob's Trouble. It is during this time that the companion must choose a side as well. Does the companion stand back and observe or do they link with the Chosen? If they decide to stand on the side line, then when the Israelites return to their land the answer will be similar to the Messiah's response to those who did not cling to him.

But whoever denies Me before men will be denied before the angels of Elohim.

Luke 12:9

The picture of the rejection of Yah's people is the same as the stone that the builder rejected. To join in the family, there must also be the placing of the chief cornerstone back in its place. This is not just the picture of the Messiah, but that of the whole family. It is the word אבן (*eben*). The *aleph* represents the father. The *bet* is a picture of the house, and the final *nun* is the seed. All of these elements must be in place, and it is through these elements that the truth of Torah is founded: Elohim, the land, and the SEED. If a person is not willing to join the chief cornerstone, they are not a companion.

It is only through this method that there will be harmony. It is important that each person does their part similar to the cosmic soccer game. It is through the symbiotic relationship that this positive union functions. When the Israelites who are spread to the four corners of the earth are given back their inheritance, it is prophesied that the Gentile or the companion will grab His garment and ask to return with Him. This is yet to happen, and cannot occur if the companion has actively participated as the oppressor. Can a people slay the children of Elohim and hold themselves not guilty of the blood that has been spilled or are they spiritually marked, like Cain, because of their hate for whom Yah has chosen? A believer is supposed to be a companion to the Children of Israel. No matter what the faith is, there is always the recognition of who the children of Yah are.

Many find the truth of Yah's Chosen People as a way to reverse racism or bondage exhibited against one group, and then place it on another people in a strange type of revenge. While this is how man's mind perceives the truth, it is not the way of the Highest. Nothing that Yah has set in place and called a blessing should be seen as anything other than that. It is not a matter of error on the Creator's part for the order He set in place, but rather it is a divine privilege that can be beautifully experienced if humanity only changed its attitude about how Yah has chosen to bless them individually and collectively. The blessing of an elect does not stop with the blood-borne of Israel but is fully understood only with their counterpart or companions. Scripture speaks of this companion, and it is with a proper Hebraic understanding that the function of the companion comes forth and the complete picture of redemption can be seen. Anything outside of the Word of Yah is divisive, and if we do not acknowledge this, then we will be continually divided.

A companion in Hebrew is חבר (*chabar*) the two-letter root of this word is חב. The two-letter root is comprised of a *het* and a *bet* which combined means "wall of the house." The walls of the house surround the family and act as a refuge and a place of hiding from an unfavorable circumstance or person. This hiding place can be seen as the arms where one is protected and cherished. When this word is viewed in its three-letter form, the Scriptural context that is seen in the book of Ezekiel is given new light. The idea is a companion or one who, in the Hebraic sense, is coupled and bound. This is a unity that is built off an important cooperative relationship.

Thus says Yahuah GOD, "Behold, I will lift up My hand to the nations And set up My standard to the peoples; And they will bring your sons in their bosom, And your daughters will be carried on their shoulders.

Isaiah 49:22

"Kings will be your guardians, And their princesses your nurses. They will bow down to you with their faces to the earth And lick the dust of your feet; And you will know that I am Yahuah; Those who hopefully wait for Me will not be put to shame.

Isaiah 49:23

"Surely the coastlands will wait for Me; And the ships of Tarshish will come first, To bring your sons from afar, Their silver and their gold with them, For the name of Yahuah your Elohim, And for the Holy One of Israel because He has glorified you.

Isaiah 60:9

Foreigners will build up your walls, And their kings will minister to you; For in My wrath I struck you, And in My favor I have had compassion on you.

Isaiah 60:10

Even with all of the atrocities seen above, there is still the option to turn. Many people will want to disagree and for a good reason after seeing the images above. But just like every other story of redemption, there is also one for those who want to turn from their wickedness and sojourn amongst the Israelites by the mercy of their Elohim. The most famous story of this is the story of Jonah. Jonah was a prophet who was called by Yah to speak to a nation who hated and abused the Children of Israel. The Ninevites were worshippers of the god, dagon. If you have seen the fish that is used to represent Christianity, then you know which god dagon is. These people and their god were very instrumental in luring the Children of Yah into idolatry as well as persecuting them. Historically, Ninevah, the capital city of Assyria, was home to a hostile people known for their ruthlessness and persecution of the Israelites. The story of Jonah is a perfect example of His non-discriminatory message. Yah is an Elohim of judgment, but He always gives space and time to repent. This is the grace of Yah. The grace of Yah allows the generation who did not participate in the sins of their fathers, but who are obliviously benefiting from their evil, the opportunity to enter into the tent.

> *And should not I spare Nineveh, that great city, wherein are more than sixscore thousand persons that cannot discern between their right hand and their left hand;*

Jonah 4:11

If Yah extended repentance and salvation to Sodom and Nineveh, He would also do the same with the daughter of Babylon (America) to give those who will turn the opportunity. Yahuah tells Jonah to go and preach to the Ninevites, and Jonah refused because they were responsible for great atrocities against the Hebrews. Jonah eventually states why he does not want to go by saying "that if he preaches they will repent and Yah will save them." Jonah's fear is inherently the same fear and anger that many Hebrews have today. The emotion is evoked by the thought of those who have offended simply coming into the "house" and allowing them to be cleared of their offenses. But rest assured that admission into the House carries prerequisites and restitution for the offense to our Abba for the mistreatment of His Children. For the nations who have offended and want to escape judgment, they have to do as the Ninevites and be willing to repent and turn from their wickedness and acknowledge the Creator and His People. They must turn away from their mistreatment. If this is not the route that the nations are willing to take then like Assyria and all other nations who rejected the salvation of Yah through His messenger and repentance of their wickedness to His People, these are some of the consequences:

"For the nation and the kingdom which will not serve you will perish, And the nations will be utterly ruined.

Isaiah 60:12

"But if they will not listen, then I will uproot that nation, uproot and destroy it," declares Yahuah.

Jeremiah 12:17

The whole purpose of returning to our Hebrew roots and learning the language is so that we can become one. The natural seed is the physical manifestation of the unseen spiritual seed which is the power of the natural seed. We must align ourselves with the will of the universe and to the Law that governs and orders its function. By operating in our purpose, we are responding to the divine call of the universe for harmony and balance. It is the process of restoration. As we are restored the rest of the world, and its elements rejoice.

For the eagerly expecting creation awaits eagerly the revelation of the sons of Elohim.

Romans 8:19

[כ]

The Two Sticks

Jeremiah 37:17-28

The word of Yahuah came again unto me, saying, Moreover, thou son of man, take thee one stick, and write upon it, For Judah, and for the Children of Israel his companions: then take another stick, and write upon it, For Joseph, the stick of Ephraim and for all the house of Israel his companions:

And join them one to another into one stick; and they shall become one in thine hand.

And when the children of thy people shall speak unto thee, saying, Wilt thou not shew us what thou meanest by these?

Say unto them, Thus saith Yahuah ELOHIM; Behold, I will take the stick of Joseph, which is in the hand of Ephraim, and the tribes of Israel his fellows, and will put them with him, even with the stick of Judah, and make them one stick, and they shall be one in mine hand.

And the sticks whereon thou writest shall be in thine hand before their eyes.

And say unto them, Thus saith Yahuah ELOHIM; *Behold, I will take the Children of Israel from among the heathen, whither they be gone, and will gather them on every side, and bring them into their own land:*

And I will make them one nation in the land upon the mountains of Israel; and one king shall be king to them all: and they shall be no more two nations, neither shall they be divided into two kingdoms any more at all.

Neither shall they defile themselves any more with their idols, nor with their detestable things, nor with any of their transgressions: but I will save them out of all their dwelling places, wherein they have sinned, and will cleanse them: so shall they be my people, and I will be their Elohim.

And David my servant shall be king over them; and they all shall have one shepherd: they shall also walk in my judgments, and observe my statutes, and do them.

And they shall dwell in the land that I have given unto Jacob my servant, wherein your fathers have dwelt; and they shall dwell therein, even they, and their children, and their children's children for ever: and my servant David shall be their prince forever.

Moreover, I will make a covenant of peace with them; it shall be an everlasting covenant with them: and I will place them, and multiply them, and will set my sanctuary in the midst of them for evermore.

My tabernacle also shall be with them: yea, I will be their Elohim, and they shall be my people.

And the heathen shall know that I Yahuah do sanctify Israel, when my sanctuary shall be in the midst of them for evermore.

The Scripture says that Judah has been dispersed and Israel has been out-casted. These two groups and their companions will be those who will be re-gathered in the day when Elohim takes them and makes them one nation.

Who is Judah? Who is Ephraim?

Judah is the group who has been dispersed, or in the Hebrew sense, smashed like a pot and scattered; and Israel has been taken and pushed or driven out. It is prophesied that in the last days that the Highest will gather His Children from the four corners of the Earth and will bring them back into their land. I believe that we are nearing that time and that repentance is the first step toward preparation. If you do not know where you stand regarding your Covenant with Yahuah or His Children now is a good time to begin introspection. I recommend trying the truth for yourself and standing firm on your convictions. The Highest said that He would not utterly destroy the Children of Israel; but that He would leave a remnant. In these current times, it is the Remnant who will be brought back and redeemed from the lands of the wicked. Yah has not forsaken His people neither has He forgot His promises. I know many in these perilous times may be asking, where is the Father? However, my prayer is that as you search through and try the information laid out, you will see that He has never left; but that He is only waiting for the ripe harvest of the fruit of His choice vine to rise and accept their true place in the Earth. As we walk in obedience, eagerly waiting to see the two sticks and their companions becoming one, let us turn back with our whole hearts. Just as our cry was heard from beneath the hot sun of Mitzraim, our voices likewise will be heard from the land of our captivity in modern-day Egypt. Though we are free from chains, it is now time for the release from prison in our minds and our unwillingness to fully submit to the Father. It is only then that Yah will return the Children whom He calls His possession to their rightful place. You are the Set-Apart People who the world is waiting for. It is you who He has loved, and in just a little while, the world will see the light on a hill.

Thank you, Abba Yah for Your promise to make us one nation again, and for not putting out the smoking wick. In this last day, as a nation in captivity, we repent and pray that You send Your Ruach (breath) over these dry bones so that they may live and testify of a day greater than the exit from Egypt. Thank You for the preservation of your Remnant. Amen.

Therefore look, days are coming,' declares Yahuah, 'and it will no longer be said, "As Yahuah lives, who led up the Israelites from the land of Egypt," but only "As Yahuah lives, who led up the Israelites from the land of the north, and from all the lands where he had driven them," for I will bring them back to their ground that I gave to their ancestors.

Jeremiah 16:14-15

Save us, O Yahuah our Elohim, And gather us from among the nations, To give thanks to Your holy name And glory in Your praise.

Psalm 106:47

Then it will happen on that day that Yahuah Will again recover the second time with His hand The remnant of His people, who will remain, From Assyria, Egypt, Pathros, Cush, Elam, Shinar, Hamath, And from the islands of the sea.

Isaiah 11:11

When Yahuah will have compassion on Jacob and again choose Israel, and settle them in their own land, then strangers will join them and attach themselves to the house of Jacob.

Isaiah 14:1

"In those days the house of Judah will walk with the house of Israel, and they will come together from the land of the north to the land that I gave your fathers as an inheritance.

Jeremiah 3:18

"Therefore behold, the days are coming," declares Yahuah, "when they will no longer say, 'As Yahuah lives, who brought up the sons of Israel from the land of Egypt,

Jeremiah 23:7

but, 'As Yahuah lives, who brought up and led back the descendants of the household of Israel from the north land and from all the countries where I had driven them.' Then they will live on their own soil."

Jeremiah 23:8

'I will be found by you,' declares Yahuah, 'and I will restore your fortunes and will gather you from *all the nations and from all the places where I have driven you,' declares Yahuah, 'and I will bring you back to the place from where I sent you into exile.'*

Jeremiah 29:14

'For behold, days are coming,' declares Yahuah, 'when I will restore the fortunes of My people Israel and Judah.' Yahuah says, 'I will also bring them back to the land that I gave to their forefathers and they shall possess it.'"

Jeremiah 30:3

"Behold, I will gather them out of all the lands to which I have driven them in My anger, in My wrath and in great indignation; and I will bring them back to this place and make them dwell in safety.

Jeremiah 32:37

Now in that day the remnant of Israel, and those of the house of Jacob who have escaped, will never again rely on the one who struck them, but will truly rely on Yahuah, the Holy One of Israel.

Isaiah10:20

And there will be a highway from Assyria For the remnant of His people who will be left, Just as there was for Israel In the day that they came up out of the land of Egypt.

Isaiah 11:16

Thus Yahuah will make Himself known to Egypt, and the Egyptians will know Yahuah in that day. They will even worship with sacrifice and offering, and will make a vow to Yahuah and perform it.

Isaiah 19:21

For I will take you from among the heathen, and gather you out of all countries, and will bring you into your own land.

Ezekiel 36:24

"Kings will be your guardians, And their princesses your nurses. They will bow down to you with their faces to the Earth And lick the dust of your feet; And you will know that I am Yahuah; Those who hopefully wait for Me will not be put to shame.

Isaiah 49:23

"The sons of those who afflicted you will come bowing to you, And all those who despised you will bow themselves at the soles of your feet; And they will call you the city of Yahuah, The Zion of the Holy One of Israel.

Isaiah 60:14

[ל]

The Redemption

The cyclical nature of Biblical history and prophecy must be taken into consideration as we deal with who the Children of Yah are as well as their function in America and the world. The nature of prophecy is to line up with words of the Creator and His will for humanity. Anything that deviates from His order must be rejected. In dealing with the captivity and identity of the Children of Yah in America, it is important that the issue is viewed separately from the popular notion that this prophecy has been fulfilled, and rather is looked at through the historical lens of the Children of Israel and their other Hebrew family members. It is important to note that just because something seems to come to pass about Biblical prophecy does not mean that the action fits all of the requirements. The Scriptures deal with a concept called progressive revelation which is consistent with the adage that "hindsight is 20/20." In the post-prophetic side of Scripture, it is easier to see what things meant and how they can be appropriated in modern times. The basis for prophecy and testing its validity can be found in Deuteronomy 13. The reason why failed prophecy is exposed in such a "harsh" manner is that of its deceptive nature and how it causes idolatry and a falling away from the truth.

If there arise among you a prophet, or a dreamer of dreams, and giveth thee a sign or a wonder, And the sign or the wonder come to pass, whereof he spake unto thee, saying, let us go after other gods, which thou hast not known, and let us serve them; Thou shalt not hearken unto the words of that prophet, or that dreamer of dreams: for Yahuah your Elohim proveth you, to know whether ye love Yahuah your Elohim with all your heart and with all your soul. Ye shall walk after Yahuah your Elohim, and fear him, and keep his commandments, and obey his

*voice, and ye shall serve him, and cleave unto him.
And that prophet, or that dreamer of dreams, shall be
put to death; because he hath spoken to turn you
away from Yahuah your Elohim, which brought you
out of the land of Egypt, and redeemed you out of the
house of bondage, to thrust thee out of the way which
Yahuah thy Elohim commanded thee to walk in. So
shalt thou put the evil away from the midst of thee.*

Deuteronomy 13:5

Throughout history, the enslavement and
selling of the Children of Yah have always
followed the same pattern and has happened at the
hand of the same people. This can be seen as far
back as Genesis 37:27-28. The picture of the nations
and the captivity of the People of Yah paralleled
with how Joseph's brothers were instrumental in
him being sold into slavery; which in turn, reveals
a future look at the bonding and relationships
between tribes. Joseph's enslavement is a picture
very consistent with the evidence of the Trans-
Atlantic Slave Trade. It is often the nature of
historians who seek to separate the melanated

races to cause people to err in thinking that there was no relation between those who sold the "Blacks" into slavery and the Native dark-skinned people of Africa. This cannot be further from the truth. In the story of Joseph, it was the Egyptian (Hamitic) Hebrews known as Ishmaelites, and the Arab/ Palestinian (Shemetic) Hebrews called Midianites, who played the role of the merchant and slave traders to take Joseph in the house of bondage Mitzraim (Egypt). All three of these groups: The Ishmaelites, the Midianites, and the Israelites each have a common ancestor in Abraham. This does not mean that all Hamites are Hebrews. Likewise, it does not make all Hebrews Israelites, but it is simply to note that those who had a hand in the intracontinental slave trade were, in fact, some way linked to the Hebrew Israelites, revealing that they also knew who exactly they were selling when they sold them. This brings up the obvious parallel between the Trans-Atlantic Slave Trade and how the individuals involved knew who they were selling too. Psalm 83:3 tells who precisely the nations were that would conspire against the Children of Yah to remove them from their inheritance and participate in their downfall as a nation.

> *For they have consulted together with one consent: they are confederate against thee: The tabernacles of Edom, and the Ishmaelites; of Moab, and the Hagarenes; Gebal, and Ammon, and Amalek; the Philistines with the inhabitants of Tyre; Assur also is joined with them: they have holpen the children of Lot. Selah.*

Psalm 83:5-8

Each one of these nations has conspired with the nations in the removal of the Children of Yah from their borders. Each of these tribal divisions was instrumental in the killing and the enslavement of Jacob's seed to cut off the seed from remembrance. This practice is observed in the Arabian during the intracontinental slave trade in Africa. Before the Trans-Atlantic Slave Trade that included the castration of men that they captured and sold and the impregnation of the women who became sex slaves to advance their seed over that of the tribes they captured, who were more often than not Hebrew Israelite. This practice happened for centuries. In his book, <u>Babylon to Timbuktu</u>, Rudolph Windsor discussed the Muslim conquests and wars that disrupted Hebrew Israelite communities after the dispersion of the tribes from Canaan and how there was a large effort by the Muslim tribes to overtake and force conversion on the Hebrew Israelites who had been displaced from their land. There was not only a physical eradication of the seed, but also there was the blotting out of Biblical practices. Through forced conversion and replacement of birthright, through a generational removal of markers which led to a connection between Isaac and Jacob, the Hebrew was convinced that his way was the way of the heathen also. A very similar practice happened with the Hebrews when they came to the shores of the Americas where they were given Christianity which includes a variation of their belief system, yet it sought to take away the markers and both their birthright and their birthplace, thus transferring their power and position to their captors.

The reason why there is a correlation between these captivities is not coincidental, but because Yah prophesied it Himself. Genesis 15:13 is the passage that many Hebrews use to relate to the amount of time the Hebrew will spend in captivity, yet there is an even deeper understanding to be gleaned. When this verse is looked at in the original Hebrew, the reader can see that two things are happening in this passage. The first is a cyclical action related to bondage and displacement, and the second is the issue of the type of captivity. These two actions are in the parts of speech used for the words "shall be" and "afflictions." The two words in Hebrew are היה (shall be), which is used in the Qal. Imperfect third person, masculine singular and ענו Piel the perfect third person. The imperfect mood indicates an incomplete action or state. The most common use of the imperfect is when it is used for a simple action in future time. The imperfect is analogously used to express routine or customary actions in the past, present or future. The imperfect frequently expresses contingency, and English modal auxiliaries such as: may, can, shall, might, could, should, would, and perhaps are used with the verb. It is used to describe a single (as opposed to a recurrent) action in the past; it varies from the perfect by giving a more vivid and pictorial example of the action. The perfect expresses the "fact," the imperfect adds color and movement by suggesting the "process" preliminary to its completion.

The imperfect is used to express the "future," referring not only to an action which is about to be accomplished but one which has not yet begun.
In regards to the use Piel perfect third person plural utilized in the word עִנּוּ it is used to denote a promise, prophecy, and threat, it commonly means that the action of the verb is sure and imminent. Since this use is common in the prophetic writings, it is usually called the prophetic perfect. It is often translated into English as either a present or future tense verb. The perfect in Hebrew in such a case emphasizes a condition which has come to "complete existence" and realization. Finally, when the perfect occurs with the vav (ו) conjunctive prefixed, it is usually translated in the future tense.

_וַיֹּאמֶר לְאַבְרָם, יָדֹעַ תֵּדַע כִּי-גֵר **יִהְיֶה**
זַרְעֲךָ בְּאֶרֶץ לֹא לָהֶם, _וַעֲבָדוּם,
_**וְעִנּוּ** אֹתָם--אַרְבַּע מֵאוֹת, שָׁנָה.

The brief grammar lesson was to show two things about this passage: 1) The issue spoken of will be repeated and perfected and 2) The perfect tense used in the word relates to affliction. The verb form of affliction is only used in this particular form one other time, and it is found in Numbers 24:24. This verse is a prophecy by the Prophet Balaam who was sent to curse the Children of Israel, but as the story goes, when he began to lie on them, he could only tell the truth and bless them. In this particular verse the prophecy about the nation that will do the perfecting through affliction is revealed and the process in which it will be done.

And **ships** *shall come* from the coast **of Chittim,** and shall afflict Ashur, and shall afflict Eber, and he also shall perish forever. (Literally translated as "perpetually.")

Numbers 24:24

The part of the Genesis 15:13 deals directly with this nation (Chittim) and their ships (also mentioned in Deut. 28:68) that will bring affliction upon Eber (Hebrews) and Ashur (Assyrians). The nation of Chittim is what gives a final clue to the perfecting process of the Children of Yah through ships, and that can be answered in asking, who is Chittim? Through a quick genealogical analysis, Chittim is none other than the isles of the Gentiles by way of Japheth, but more specifically the Greeks and the Romans (who to the Hebrews were one nation that could be referred to interchangeably). By looking at Genesis 10, this can be easily confirmed.

Until the time of the Trans-Atlantic Slave Trade, slavery had been mainly intracontinental through a national exchange of rulership (occupation) or caravanning into captivity (walked into other nations). It was not until Chittim came with their ships that the perpetual perishing occurred for the Hebrew. Before the ships of Chittim, there was always an exchange of power between the nations that sought to occupy or take from the Israelites even until the period of the Maccabees. It was not long after 70 A.D. that the powerlessness of the remaining Hebrews of the Southern Tribe of Judah in Jerusalem was forced into Africa and toward the coast lands. Here they were continually pursued by their cousins the Ishmaelites and Midianites and eventually sold into the house of bondage through the ships of Chittim which fulfilled prophecy in spreading them and those who had been kicked out of the land (the Ten Northern Tribes) before Babylonian exile to the four corners of the world.

The same way that the world was gathered in Egypt during the famine to testify to the world about the power of Yah to bring His People out of captivity, in a similar way the scattering and gathering of His Children from the four corners of the world will be a testament. It is written, no one will even speak about the return of the captivity

from Egypt, they will now talk about the return of
His People from the four corners

> *Therefore, behold, the days come, saith Yahuah, that*
> *they shall no more say, Yahuah liveth, which*
> *brought up the Children of Israel out of the land of*
> *Egypt; But, Yahuah liveth, which brought up and*
> *which led the seed of the house of Israel out of the*
> *north country, and from all countries whither I had*
> *driven them; and they shall dwell in their own land.*

Jeremiah 23:7-9

400 Years & Jacobs Trouble

And the dragon was wroth with the woman, and went to make war with the remnant of her seed, which keep the commandments of Yah, and have the testimony of Yahusha.

Revelation 12:17

Because of the severity of erroneous interpretation and punishment that comes with making and interpreting prophecy, it is with wisdom that there will be no predicting of the time in which future events will come to pass. With that being said it serves as a valid question to explore whether or not the 400-year portion of the Genesis prophecy applies to the later or the current (spiritual & physical) Egyptian bondage. It is the opinion of the author that it is both. In the earlier Egyptian captivity some circumstances led many to believe the Hebrews in Egypt were not afflicted for 400 years, but likewise, with the Diaspora and different tribes being removed at various times to different places, it would also be hard to exclude other tribes and their longer exile. One plausible idea is that the Tribe of Judah is the timeline for all the tribes; because Judah is the Chosen from amongst the Chosen (Psalm 114:2). In Scripture, Judah has prevailed over his brother and also represents the leading population of Hebrews in the wilderness (Numbers 1:2-3, 27). It is also important to note that there is no tribe spoke of more than Judah in Scripture, there are more prophets to the Southern Kingdom, as well as all of the major reforms back to Yah's Word were led by a Judahite King. Last, but not least, is the Biblical motif of the leaders from the Tribe of Judah always have a center-stage presence in their captivity.

A very familiar story about the exiles of the Southern Kingdom is the story of Daniel, Hananiah, Mishael, and Azariah. Not only were these four men from the Tribe of Judah; but they were the most popular figures in Babylon, the same way with the American Negro. Above all the other tribes and nations, the American Negro has always been the center of the world's attention (negative or positive). Whether it is through music, sports, or oppression, the cause of the American Negro has outmoded that of the Native Americans,

Jamaicans, Negros in European nations, or Africans.

The world seems to be drawn to Judah because Judah is the Kings and Leaders of the Word by divine ordination. Scripture confirms this Tribe as a Leader and the Lawgiver of which is set in place by Yah (Psalm 60:7 and Psalm 108:8). According to the book of Numbers, Yah assigned the position of the first rank to Judah when it came to the order that they would move out of the wilderness. It would serve to reason that from the wilderness and return to captivity that this order would remain, and it is the end of Judah's captivity that would mark the return to the land. It would also be a logical deduction that because it is the Messiah that will be leading home and ruling after the last captivity, that the Tribe of the Messiah would have some rank in establishing and mobilizing home.

All that were numbered in the camp of Judah were an hundred thousand and fourscore thousand and six thousand and four hundred, throughout their armies. These shall first set forth.

Numbers 2:9

In these last days, it is important to remember the seed is the marker for future events. The seed was increased before they were taken into the land. The land is for the seed, yet simply being outside of the land does not negate the existence of the seed, and in the same respect, being in the land does not make someone the seed. The physical presence of the seed gives the marker for prophecy, especially since it is known through the cyclical nature of Scripture, that prophecy is still carried out even when the seed was removed from their land. In Babylon, the seed served as the marker for the 70-year release from captivity, likewise in this latter time, it will be the seed that will serve as the marker for the release from this final captivity.

Fear none of those things which thou shalt suffer: behold, the devil shall cast some of you into prison, that ye may be tried; and ye shall have tribulation ten days: be thou faithful unto death, and I will give thee a crown of life.

Revelation 2:10

Yet the number of the sons of Israel Will be like the sand of the sea, which cannot be measured or numbered; And in the place Where it is said to them, "You are not My people," It will be said to them, "You are the sons of the living Elohim."

Hosea 1:10

Bibliography

Benner, J. A. (2005). *The ancient Hebrew lexicon of the Bible: Hebrew letters, words and roots defined within their ancient cultural context.* College Station, TX: Virtualbookworm.com Publishing.

Clark, M., & Hirsch, S. R. (1999). *Etymological dictionary of Biblical Hebrew: Based on the commentaries of Rabbi Samson Raphael Hirsch.* Jerusalem: Feldheim Pub.

Dixon, R. B. (1923). *The Racial History of Man.* C. Scribner's Sons.

Hebrew-Greek key word study Bible: English standard version, genuine. (2013). Place of publication not identified: Amg Pubs.

Nasi, A. A. (2015, October 22). The East African Israelites of Zanjiland. Retrieved October 27, 2016, from https://arianasiresearch.wordpress.com/2015/10/22/east-african-israelites-of-zanjiland/

Windsor, R. R. (1988). *From Babylon to Timbuktu: A history of the ancient Black races including the Black Hebrews.* Phila., PA: Windsor's Golden Series Publications.